I06605871

This edition dedicated to my parents, Charlie and Mary Appice

Original oil painting of cover design: Arlene Lawin

Exclusively distributed by Hudson Music
Executive producer: Rob Wallis
Editor: Joe Bergamini
Layout & design editing: Michael Hoff

To Download Audio for this Book:
Go to: halleonard.com/mylibrary
Enter Code: 8872-5213-7584-8627

HUDSON MUSIC®

www.carmineappice.com
www.hudsonmusic.com

Contents

Contents

	Page	 Audio

CD CREDITS
CD produced by Carmine Appice for Bianic Music
Recorded at Sound Asylum
Digital editing and engineering by Steve (The Lunatic) Werbelow

FOREWORD

Welcome to the CLASSIC REALISTIC ROCK DRUM METHOD! I have added many new exercises and applications to this edition that will make it the most complete rock book ever!

All of the examples with an audio icon can be streamed or downloaded from the website indicated inside the front cover of the book.

Odd time signatures will no longer be a challenge. The 7/8 and 9/8 sections will have you playing them as easily as 4/4.

The combinations (hand and foot) section will explore more double bass (double pedal) patterns using your China cymbals in a variety of musical situations.

The play-along songs have been recorded without drums so that you can now practice and apply your favorite *Realistic Rock* patterns.

I have added more albums on my discography and updated my endorsements for you to see.

All of this, along with all of the classic exercises from the original *Realistic Rock* book and the updates, creates an exciting new dimension for you to learn how to play rock drums!

Now you can become one of the many great drummers who have gone through *Realistic Rock*—drummers like Dave Weckl, Greg Bissonnette, Vinny Appice, and Andrew Dice Clay, just to name a few.

I hope this book continues to help drummers of all ages around the world just like the original book has done in the past. Now let's ROCK!

Part 1

Key To The Book

This book should be practiced at a slow tempo, at first. Then, as it becomes easier, bring the tempo up, little by little. Every exercise in the book is in 4/4, so the 4/4 time signature at the start of each exercise has been eliminated.

At the beginning of each exercise each line is marked for easy identification.

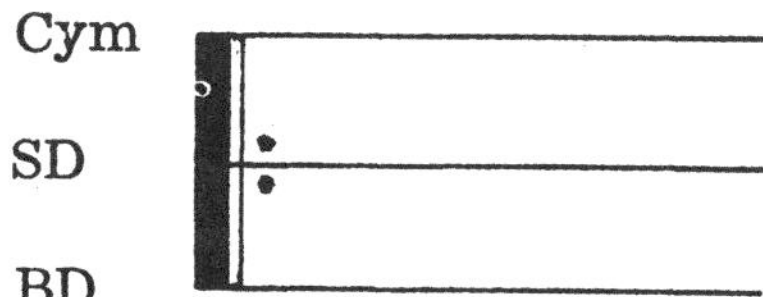

- Legend:
  - Cym = Ride Cymbal or Hi-Hat Cymbals (Either can be used . . . it is up to you, unless specified.)
  - SD = Snare Drum
  - BD = Bass Drum

At the end of each exercise is a repeat sign :‖ which means repeat once. Some exercises will be played at least eight times. The more you play the exercise, the better you'll get!

Now let's go to the note values which are used in this book!

• Note Type:		• Length of Beats:
Quarter Notes . . . . ♩	=	1 Beat
Eighth Note. . . . . ♪	=	½ Beat
Sixteenth Notes . . . . 𝅘𝅥𝅯	=	¼ Beat
Thirty-second Notes . . . . . 𝅘𝅥𝅰	=	⅛ Beat

- How to Count:
  - ♩ = 1 2 3 4
  - ♪ = 1 & 2 & 3 & 4 &
  - 𝅘𝅥𝅯 = 1 e & a 2 e & a 3 e & a 4 e & a
  - 𝅘𝅥𝅰 = No counting system; just "feel it" against the sixteenth note count.

Eighth notes are twice as fast as quarters.
Sixteenth notes are twice as fast as eighths.
Thirty-second notes are twice as fast as sixteenths—that is how to feel thirty-seconds instead of counting them. All rest values are the same and will be explained as they are used.

Part II deals with eighth notes on the cymbal, quarter and eighth notes between hand and foot. Part II is the elementary part of the book.

At the end of Part III is a 12 bar exercise. To get the feel of playing different rhythms side by side, this exercise was designed as a collage of all the rhythms played up to that point. It's a review in the form of a drum solo. You'll find such exercises at the end of each part.

If possible, all exercises should be played at the drum set to get the right rhythmic feel and the correct balance needed for tonal separation.

18 Ways To Use This Book

Here are eighteen ways to play the rhythms in this book. First play each exercise as written. Then play one of the ways shown below by matching the hand rhythms (numbers 1 - 6) with the Hi-Hat rhythms (letters A - C). Any rhythm pattern that has eighth notes on the right hand (left hand for left-handed drummers) can be varied this way.

HAND RHYTHMS	HI-HAT RHYTHMS
1. As written (right hand on cymbal)	A. Hi-Hat on quarter notes
* 2. Backwards (left hand on cymbal)	B. Hi-Hat on eighth notes
3. Right hand on quarter notes	C. Hi-Hat on "&"
* 4. Backwards on quarter notes (left hand on cymbal))	
5. Right hand on the "&"	
6. Backwards on the "&" (left hand on cymbal)	

* "Backwards": right handed drummers play left hand on the ride cymbal; left handed drummers play right hand on the ride cymbal.

EXAMPLE

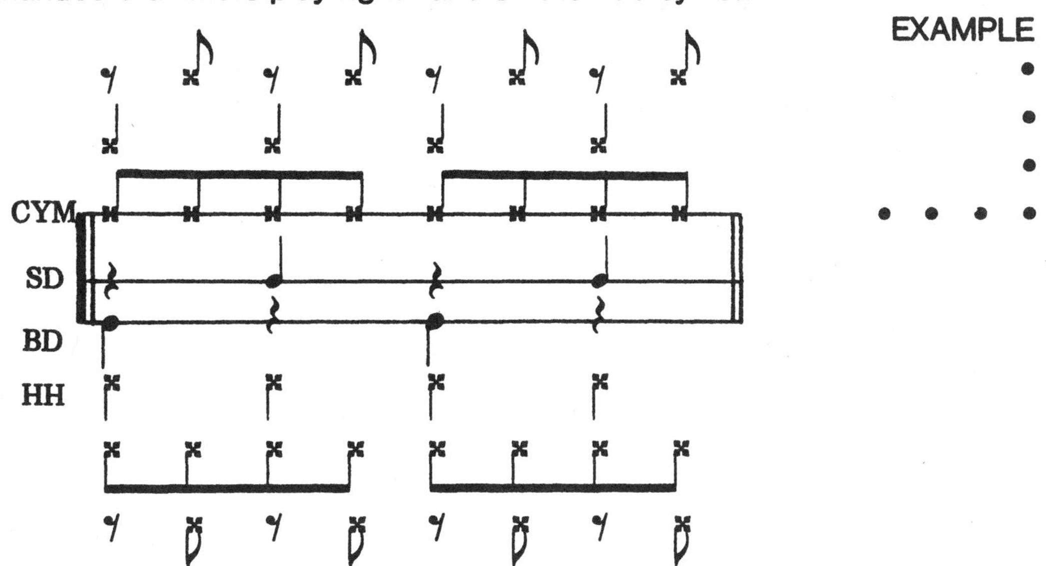

Some exercises, such as polyrhythms, cannot be varied because the ride cymbal or Hi-Hat hand is playing set patterns. For polyrhythms, play the A, B and C patterns on the Hi-Hat (worked by foot).

Part 2

Audio

Quarter Notes

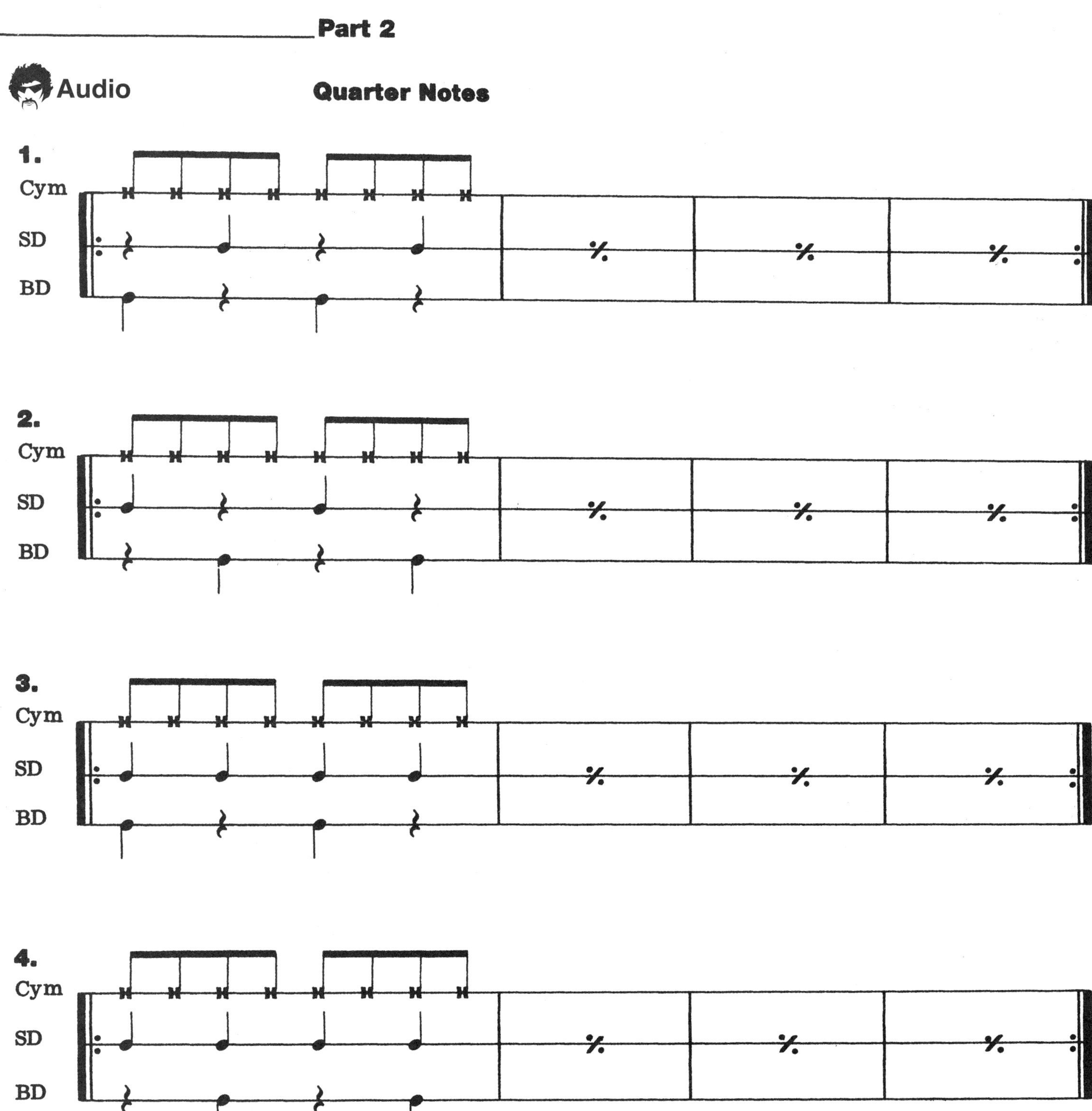

5.

Cym
SD
BD

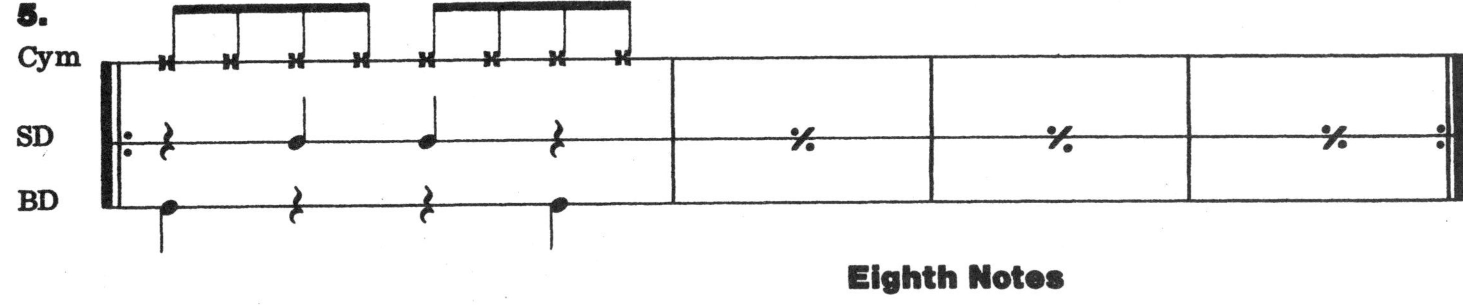

Eighth Notes

(>) = Emphasize (play louder) notes with this mark.

6.

Cym
SD
BD

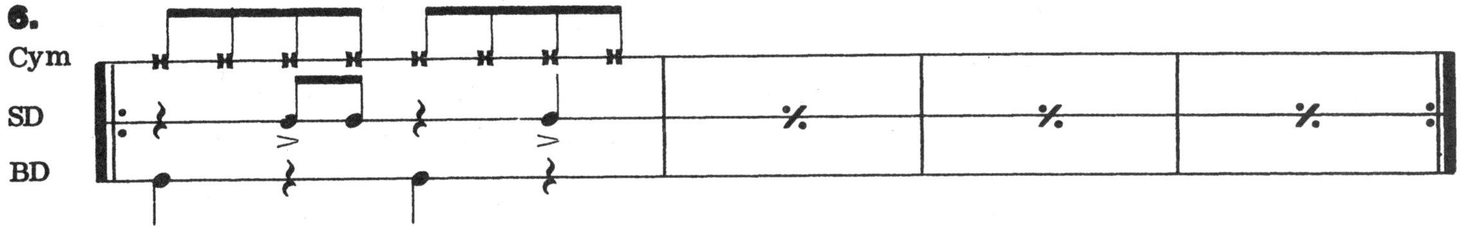

7.

Cym
SD
BD

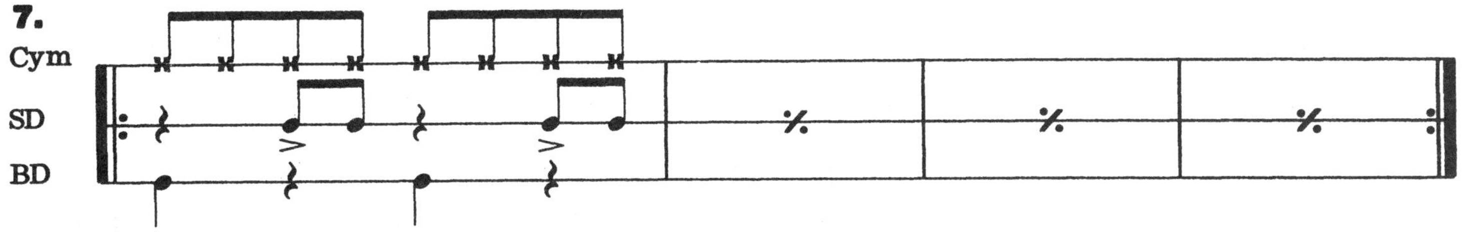

8.

Cym
SD
BD

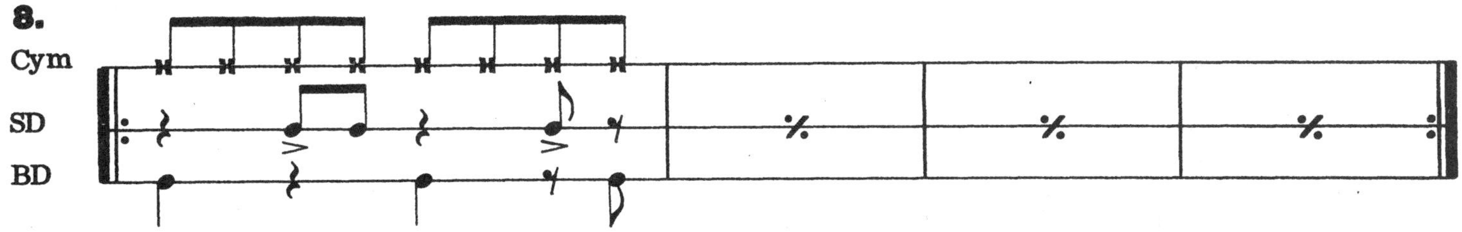

9.

Cym
SD
BD
2

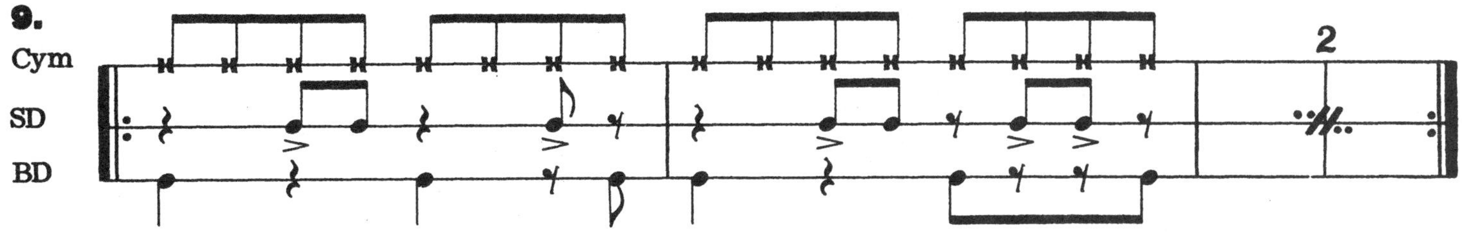

Part 3

Accented Bass Drum

In this exercise, accent the bass drum by playing on the "&" of the beat. This kind of accent is called an "off" kick.

• • • • • • • • • •

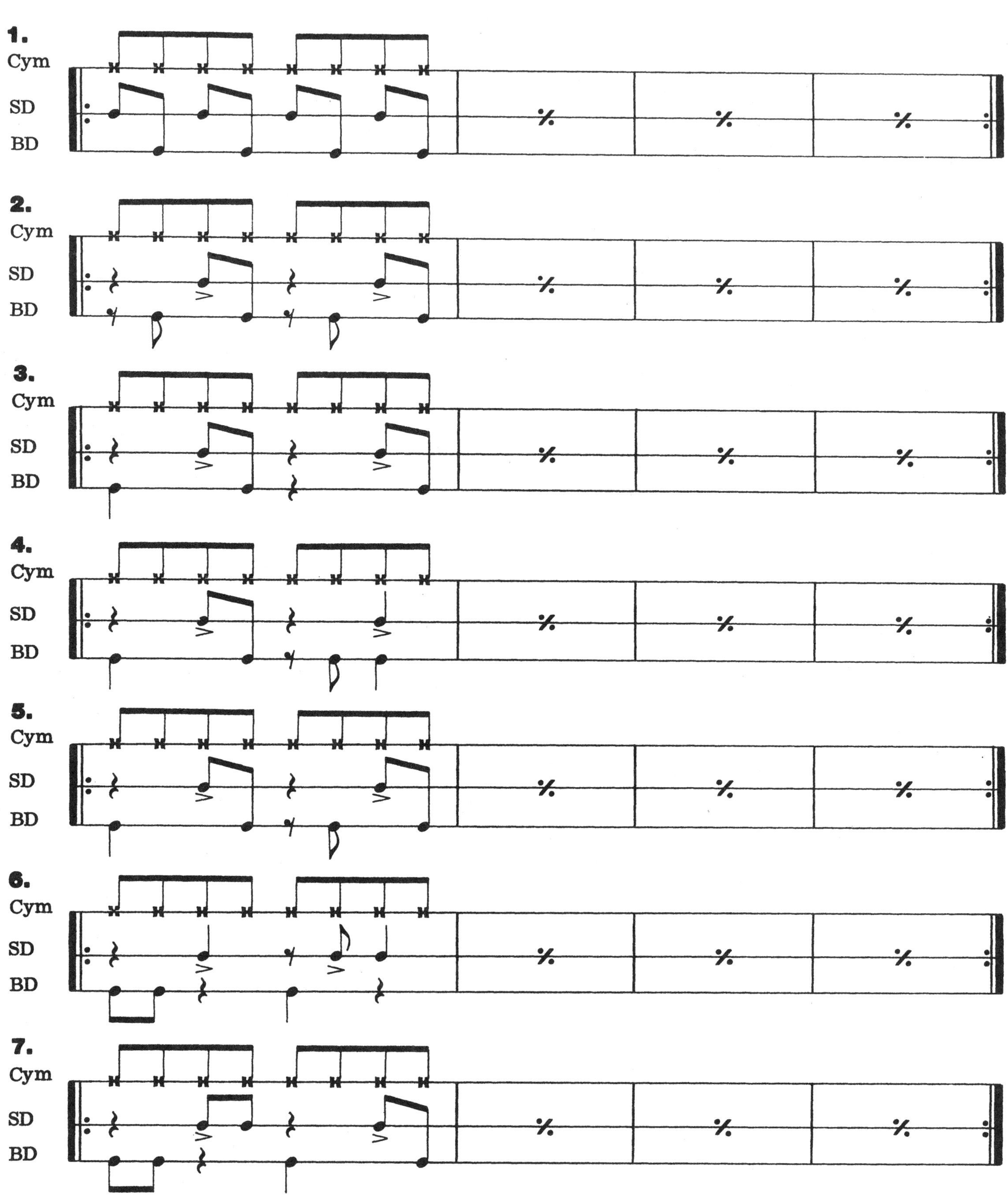
1.
Cym
SD
BD
2.
Cym
SD
BD
3.
Cym
SD
BD
4.
Cym
SD
BD
5.
Cym
SD
BD
6.
Cym
SD
BD
7.
Cym
SD
BD

Twelve Bar Exercise

Audio

This exercise is a review of the quarter and eighth note sections.

Cym

SD

BD

Part 4

Sixteenth Note Rhythms

Rock drummers rely heavily on sixteenth notes. The count for a set of 16th notes is 1 e & a. Each set of four 16th's is equal to one quarter note:

A 16th note rest has the same value as a 16th note—¼ of a beat. In this figure 1 e & a, count 1-e-&-a but hit only the last three notes. A rest can be anywhere in the figure. Eighth note rests can also appear.

This section also introduces the dotted eighth and sixteenth. The dot increases the value of the preceeding note by one half. Since an eighth note equals two sixteenth notes, a dotten eighth equals three sixteenth notes. A dotted eighth and a sixteenth add up to one beat. Count the figures like this: 1 e & a or 1 a. This rhythm is played with a bounce.

Another figure used in this section is

This is a syncopated rhythm.

Audio

Hit on 1, e. Rest on &. Hit on a.

1.

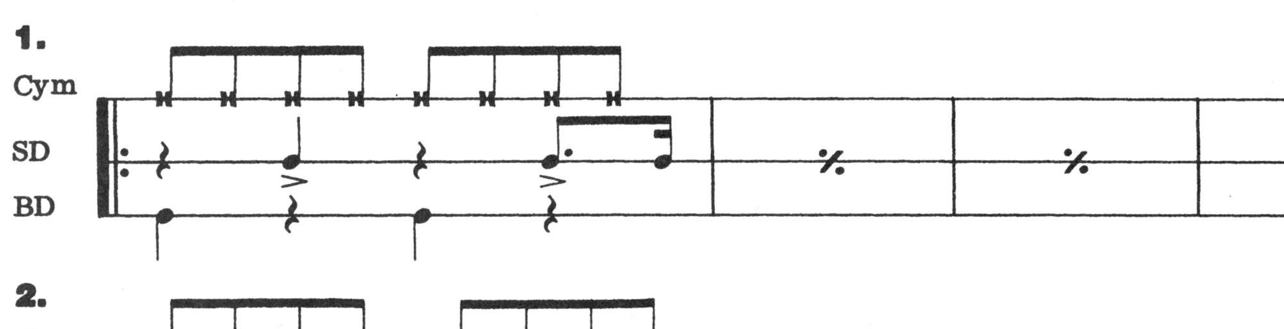

2.

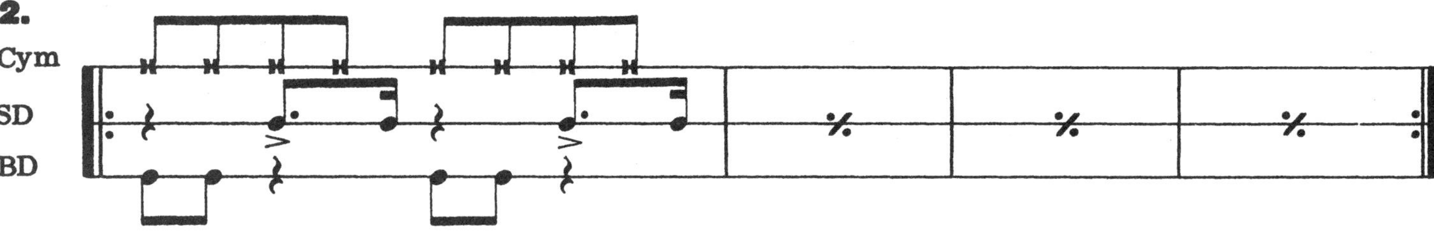

Eight Bar Exercises in Sixteenth Notes

More Sixteenths

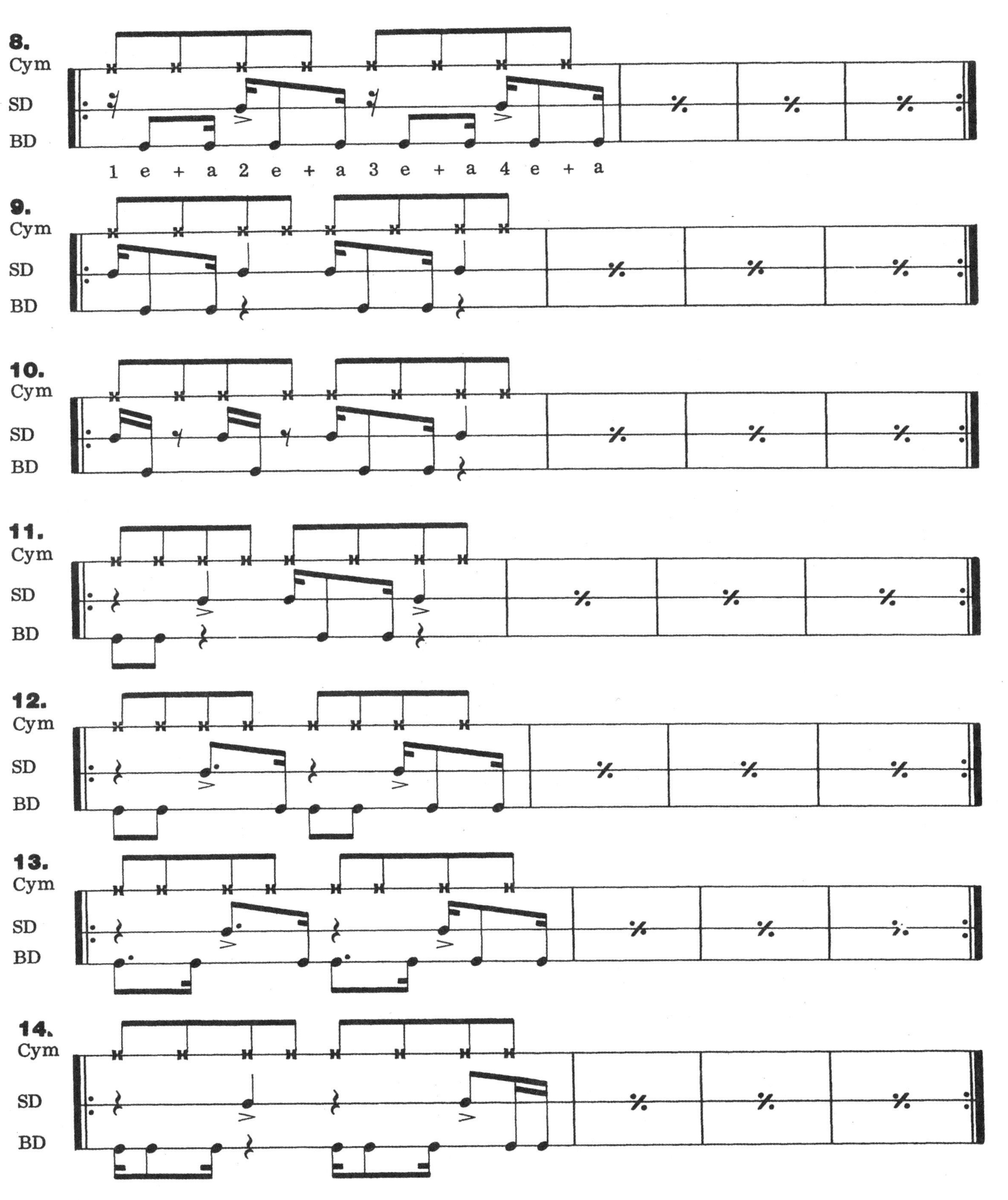
8.
Cym
SD
BD
1 e + a 2 e + a 3 e + a 4 e + a
9.
Cym
SD
BD
10.
Cym
SD
BD
11.
Cym
SD
BD
12.
Cym
SD
BD
13.
Cym
SD
BD
14.
Cym
SD
BD

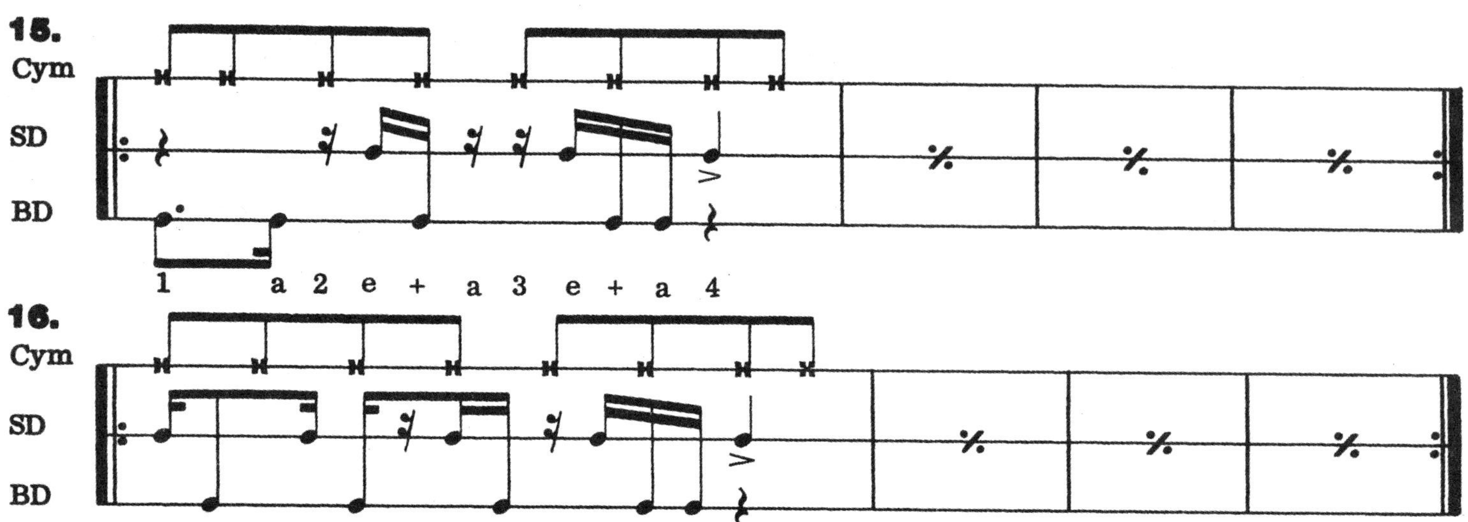

Twelve Bar Exercise — Sixteenth Notes

This exercise should be played slowly at first.

Cym

SD

BD

1 e + a

Part 5

Sixteenth Note Triplets

Audio

Sixteenth note triplets are counted: 1 ti ta + ti ta Two groups of sixteenth note triplets equal two eighth notes: 1 + The secret for reading sixteenth note triplets is simple. The first 16th note of the triplet is usually left out:

1 ti ta;

therefore, the triplet fits between the eighth notes that are being played on the Cymbal. Example:

Sixteenth note triplet figures are easy to play if this is kept in mind. The only possible problem—a fast, basic beat—can be solved by playing these exercises very slowly. Gradually increase the tempo.

1.

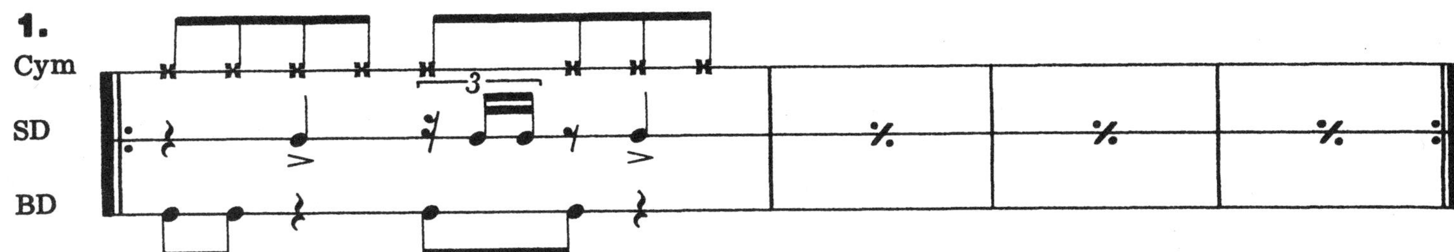

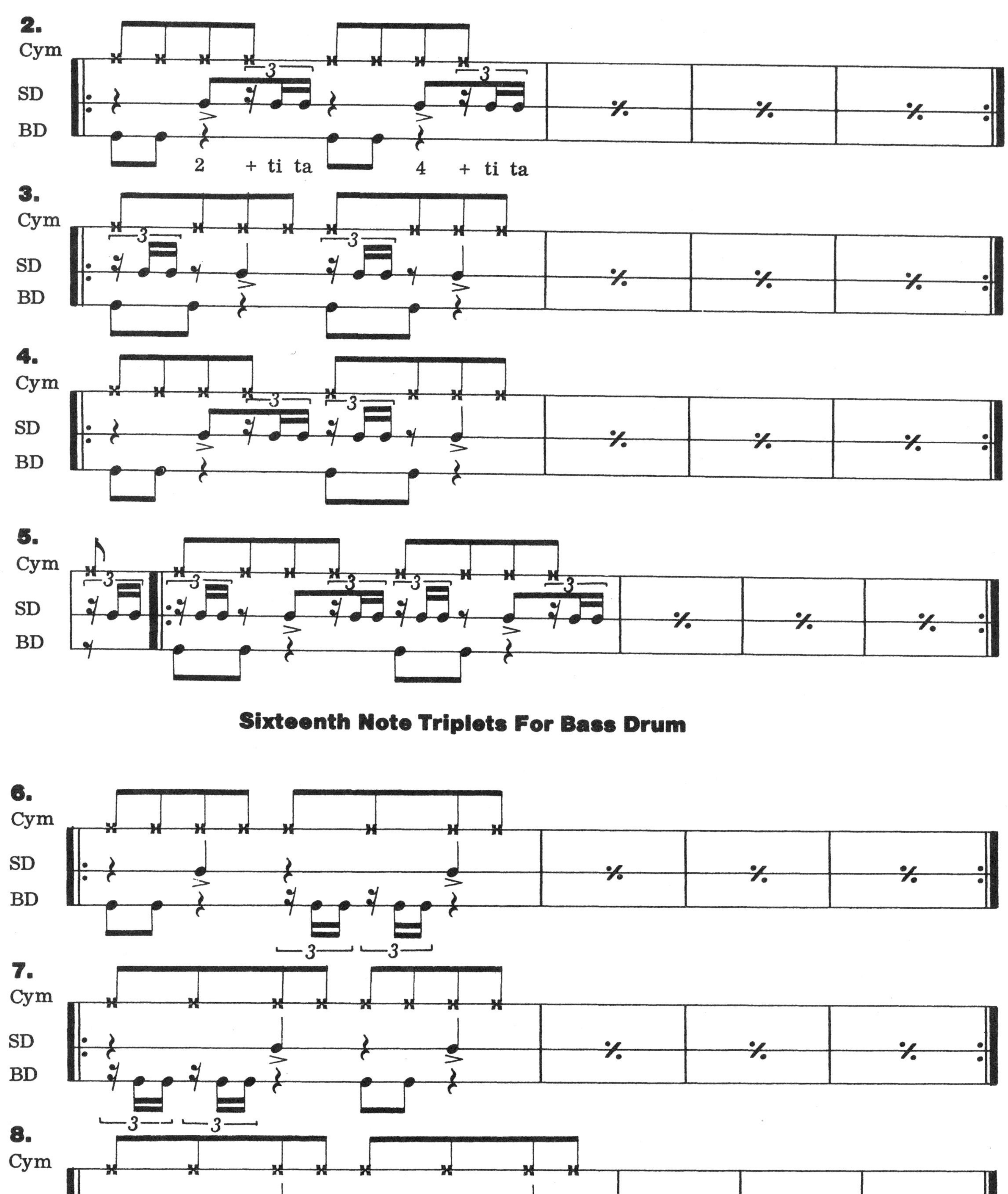
2.
Cym
SD
BD
2 + ti ta
4 + ti ta
3.
Cym
SD
BD
4.
Cym
SD
BD
5.
Cym
SD
BD
Sixteenth Note Triplets For Bass Drum
6.
Cym
SD
BD
7.
Cym
SD
BD
8.
Cym
SD
BD

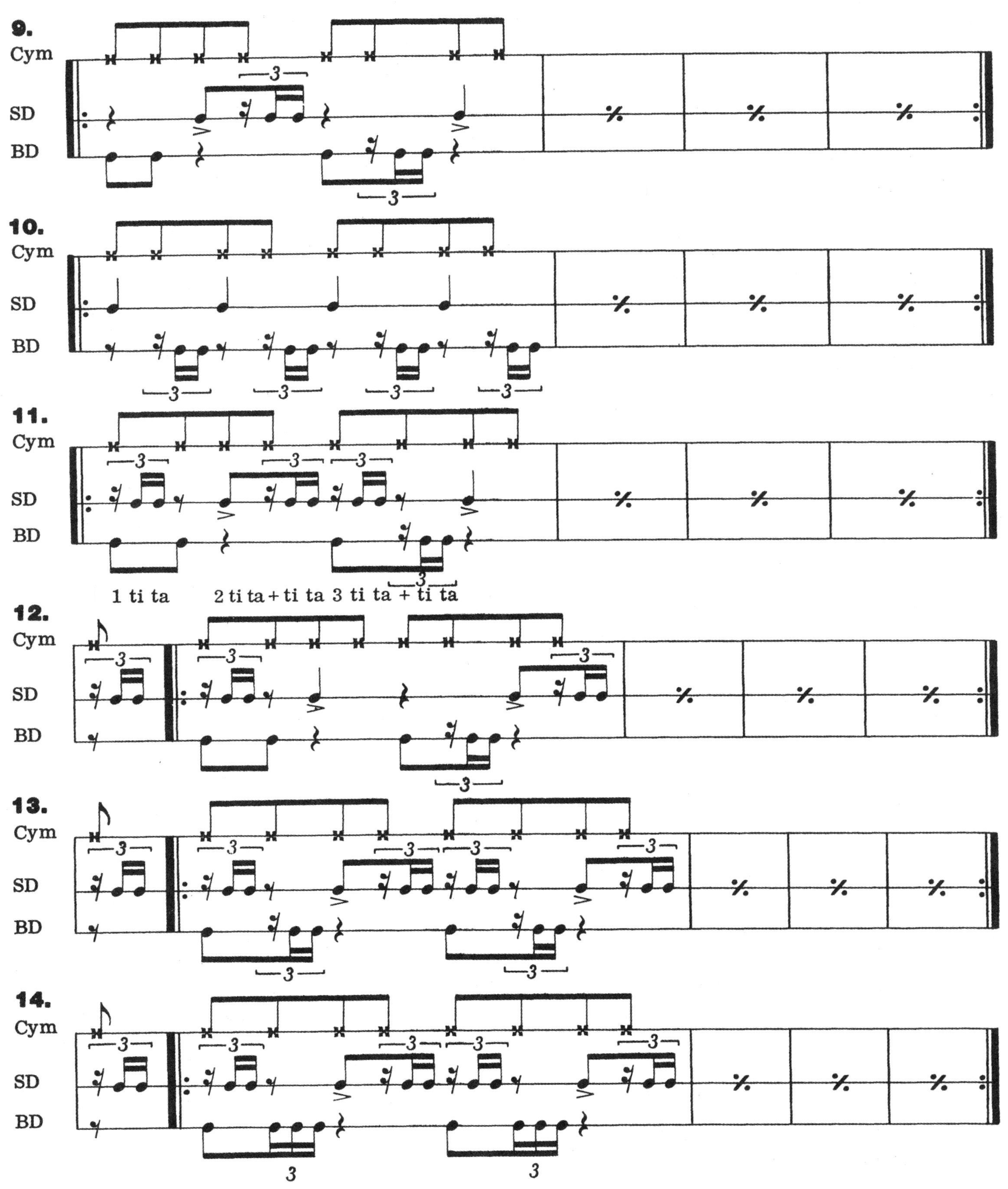
9.
Cym
SD
BD
10.
Cym
SD
BD
11.
Cym
SD
BD
1 ti ta 2 ti ta + ti ta 3 ti ta + ti ta
12.
Cym
SD
BD
13.
Cym
SD
BD
14.
Cym
SD
BD

15.

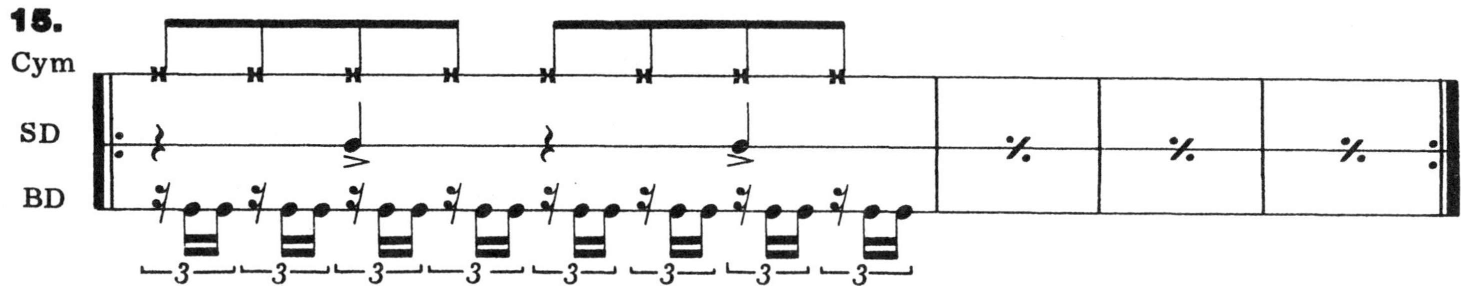

Twelve Bar Exercise

Sixteenth Note Triplet

Cym

SD

BD

The next pages will be a combination of all the rhythms learned up to this point, plus some new ones. You should be able to play these if you learned the preceding exercises.

Part 6

Review Exercises

The following exercises will develop one's ability to improvise on the rhythms previously learned. In this section the rhythms appear in 12, 14 and 16 bar exercises and solos. Play these slowly at first. Repeat at gradually faster tempos.

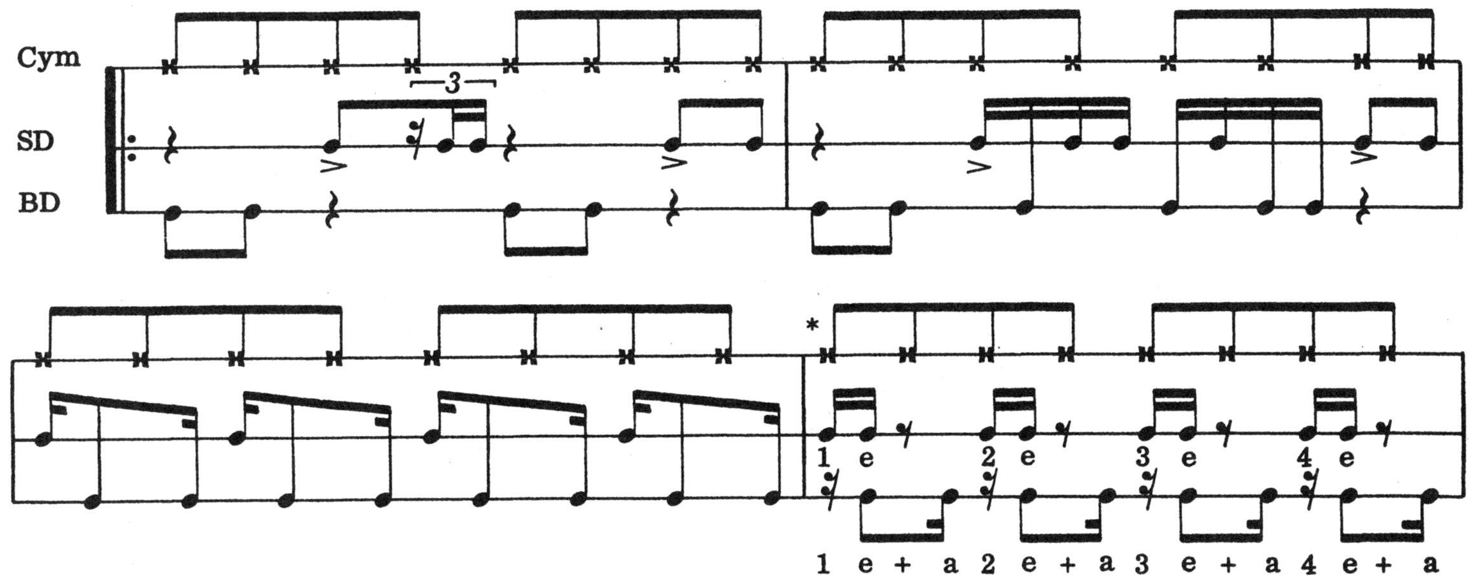

*Keep same foot rhythm as preceding measure and double snare drum figure.

1 e + a 2 e + a

Sixteen Bar Exercise

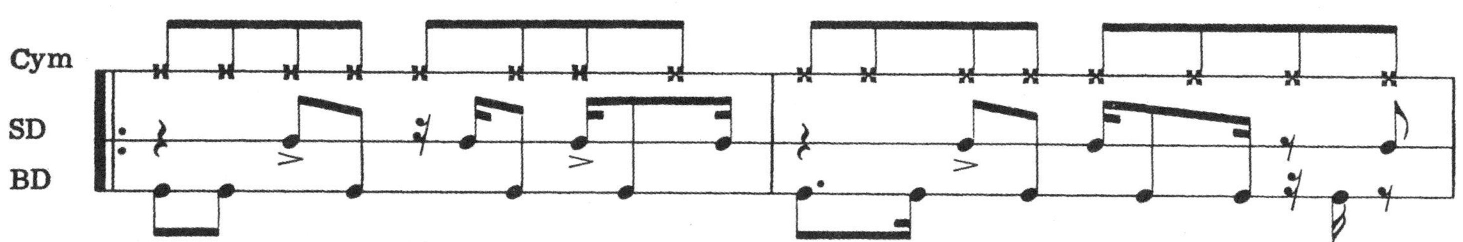

3
3
3
3

Changing Bass Drum Patterns

Sixteen Bar Solo Using Hand On 2 And 4

Steady Four On The Snare
Cym
SD
BD

Part 7

Syncopation

Syncopation is an off-beat rhythm. Beats that are not usually accented are now emphasized; the rhythm is broken up. The hard presence of the 2 & 4 after-beat disappears, but is still felt. Syncopation is used in musical styles as divergent as rhythm and blues and hard rock.

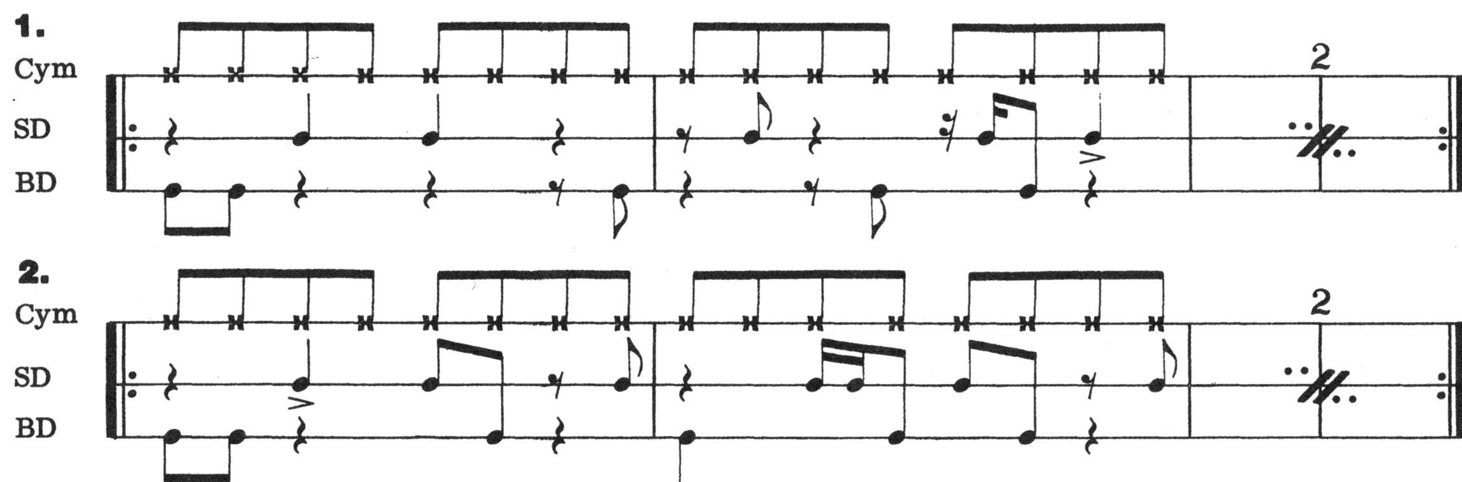

3.

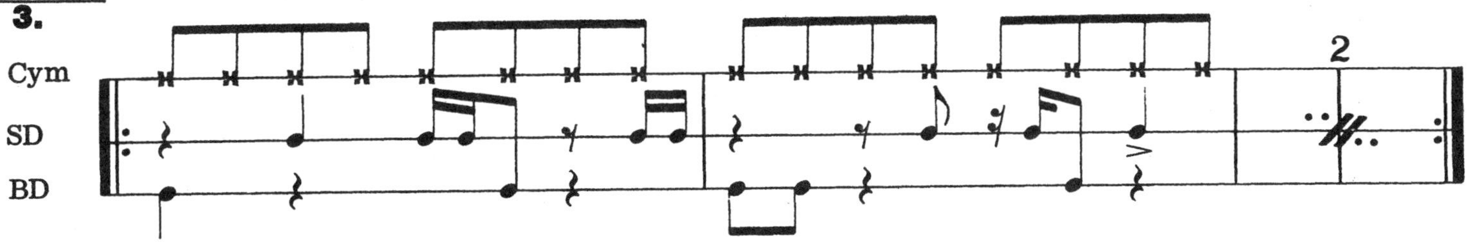

Cym
SD
BD
2

4.

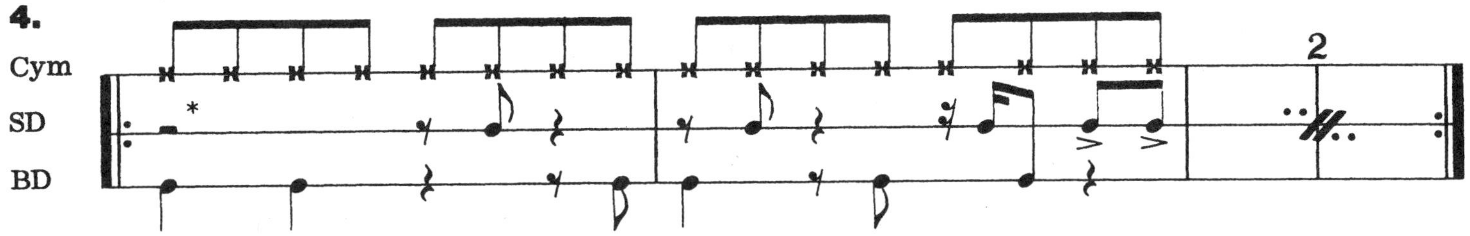

Cym
SD
BD
*
2

5.

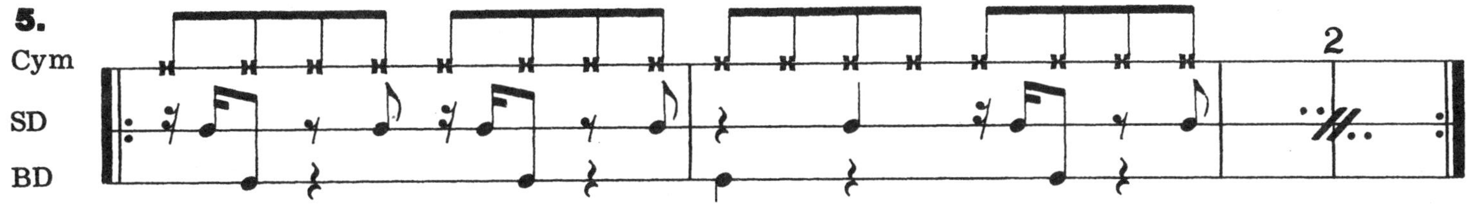

Cym
SD
BD
2

*Half note rest (▬) gets two full beat rests.

6.

Cym
SD
BD
2

7.

Cym
SD
BD
2

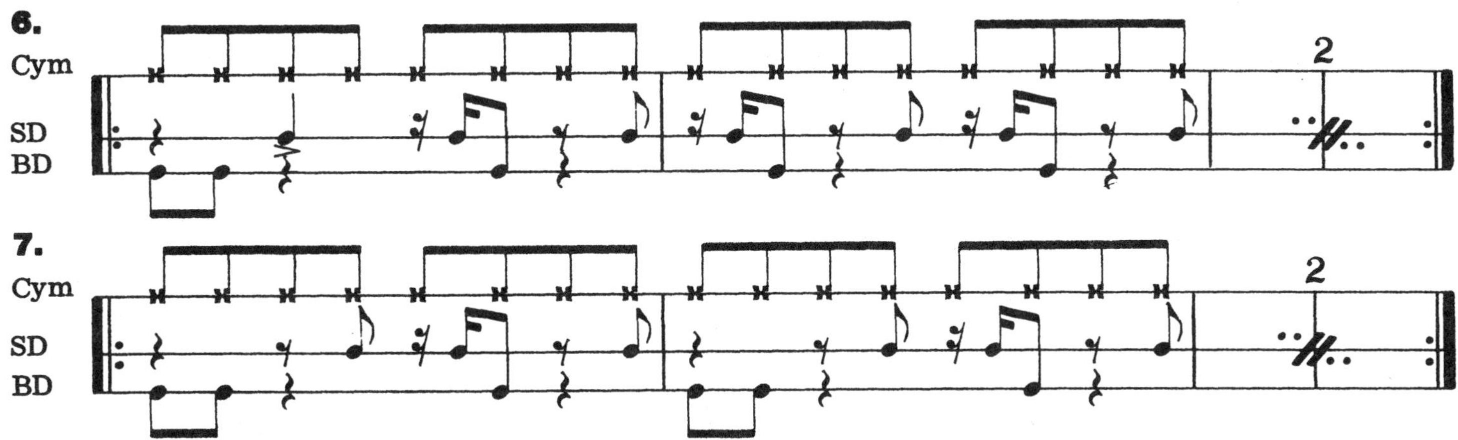

Sixteen Bar Exercise

This 16 bar exercise could easily be used as a drum break in a song with this type of feel.

Cym
SD
BD

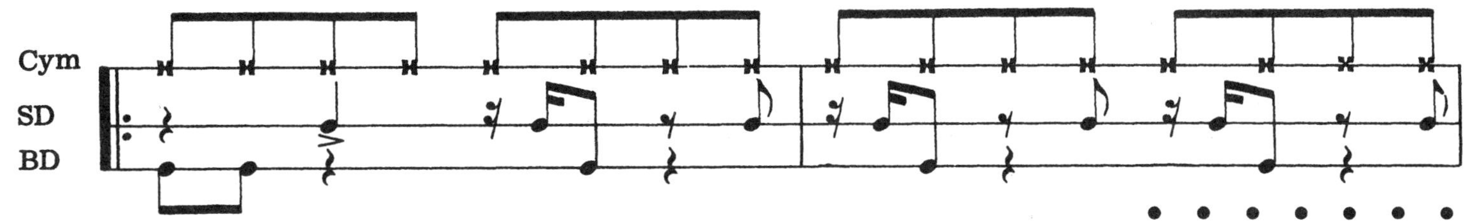

Two Bar Breaks

Syncopation is usually played in 2 to 4 measure sequences, followed by the original rhythm.

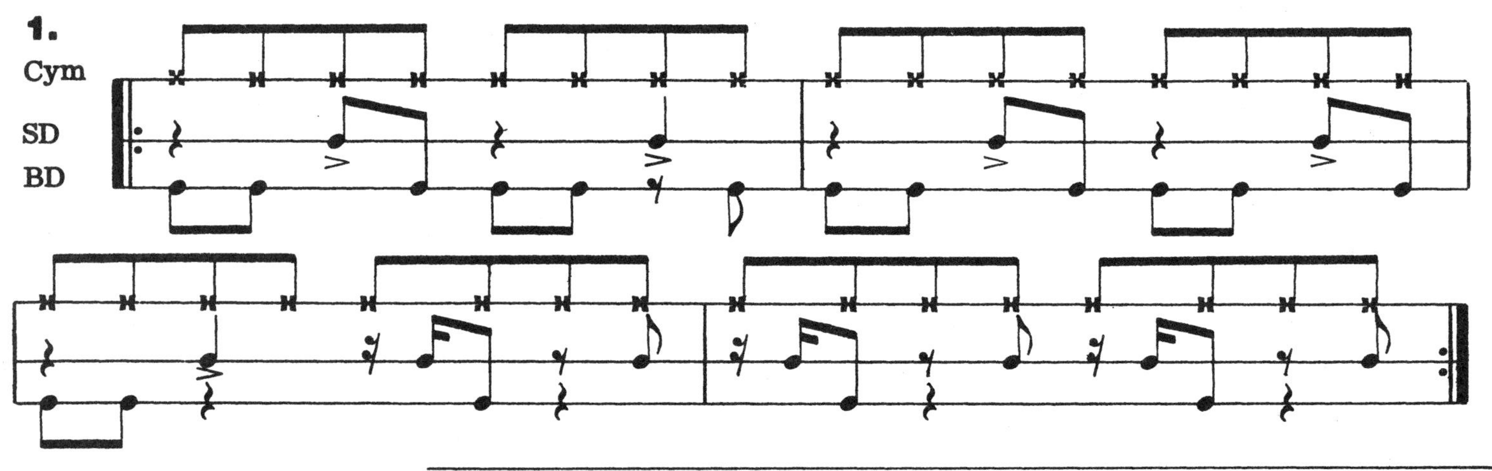

2.
Cym
SD
BD
3.
Cym
SD
BD
3
4.
Cym
SD
BD
5.
Cym
SD
BD

6.
Cym
SD
BD
7.
Cym
SD
BD
8.
Cym
SD
BD

Part 8

Hi Hat Rhythms

In recent years many original variations have been added to the standard repertoire of Hi-Hat rock rhythms. The Hi-Hat studies in parts VIII and IX will cover both the old and the new.

+ = closed
o = open

Study the vertical and horizontal relationship of the notes on all lines. Notice that as the Hi-Hat opens and closes, a more complete, rhythmic sound is created

Remember to play these slowly at first. Repeat at gradually faster tempos.

Audio

Basic Eighth Note Hi-Hat Rhythms

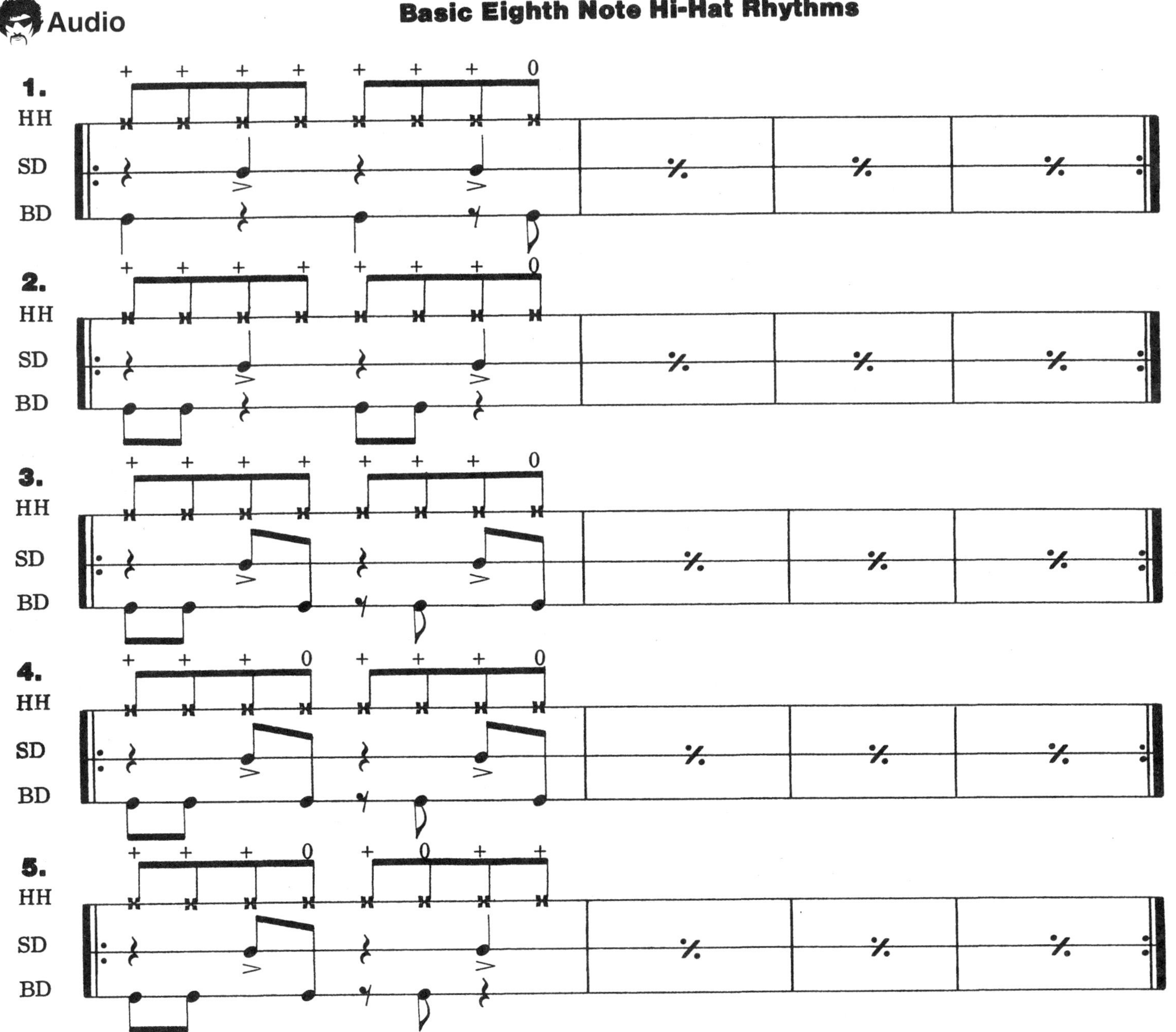

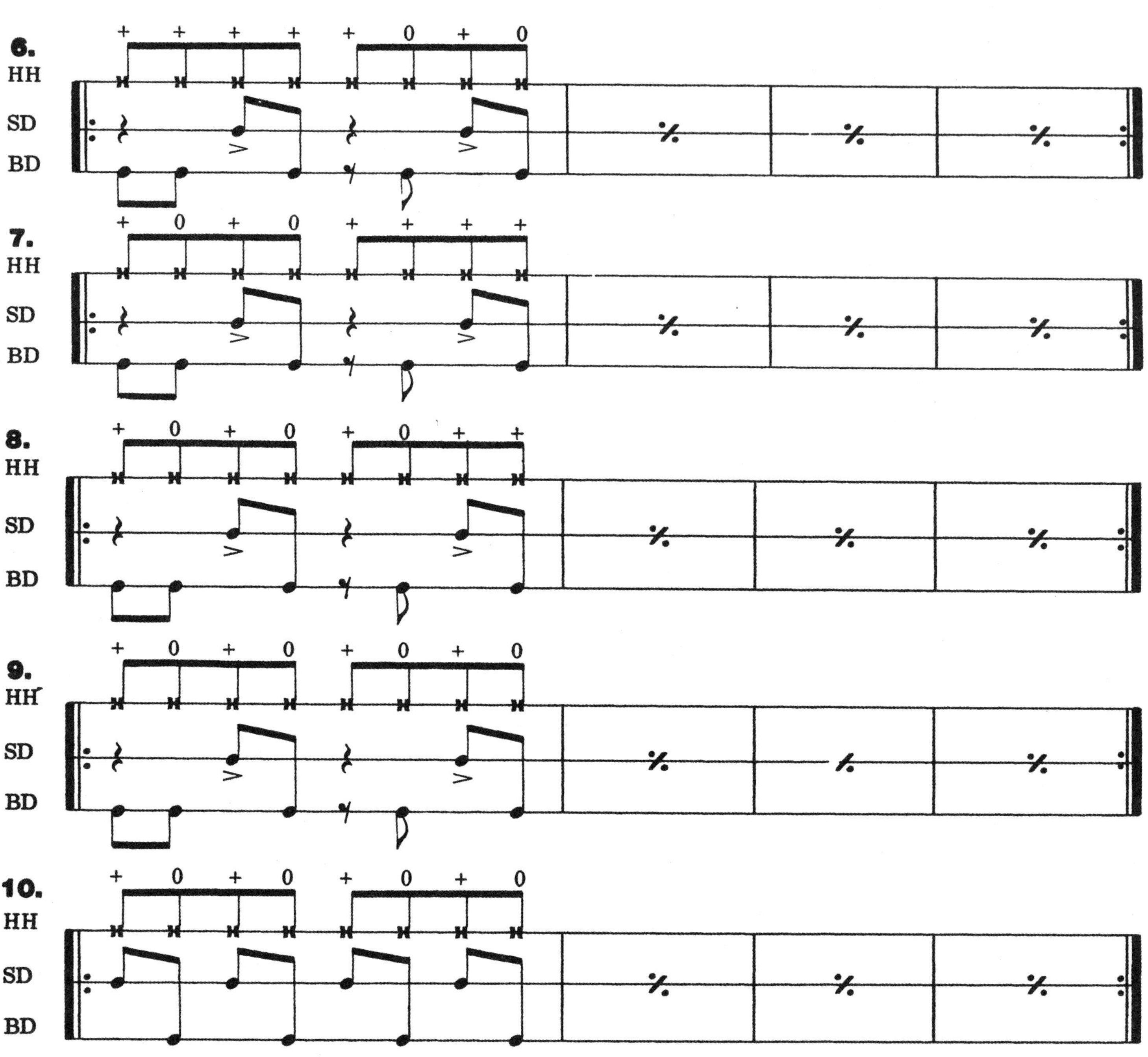

HH accents are very effective when accenting BD with it.

Slightly Syncopated

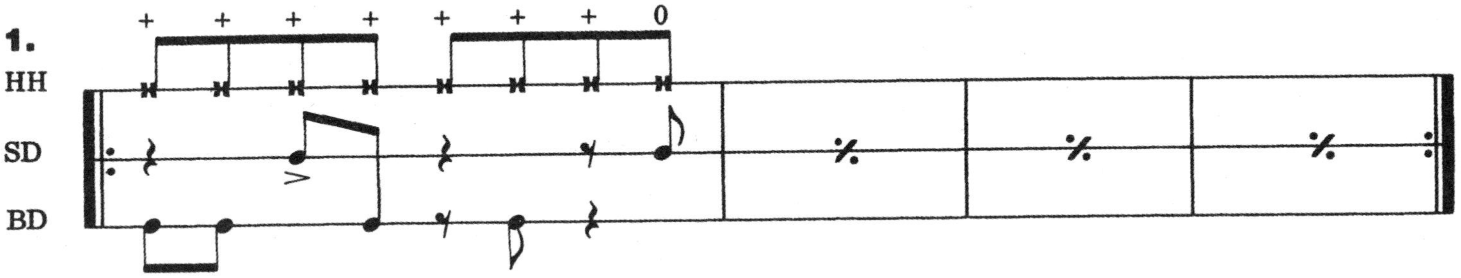

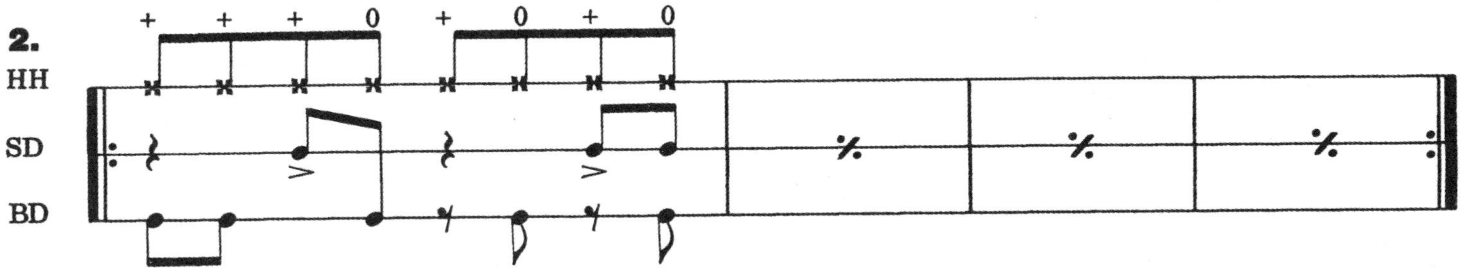

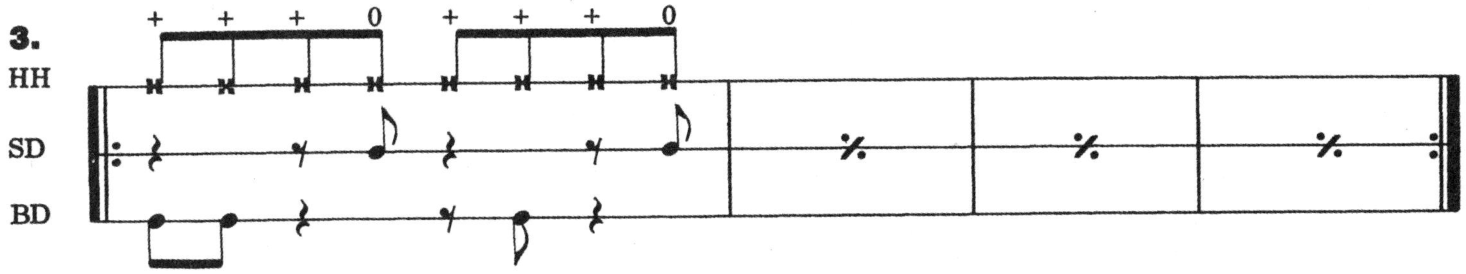

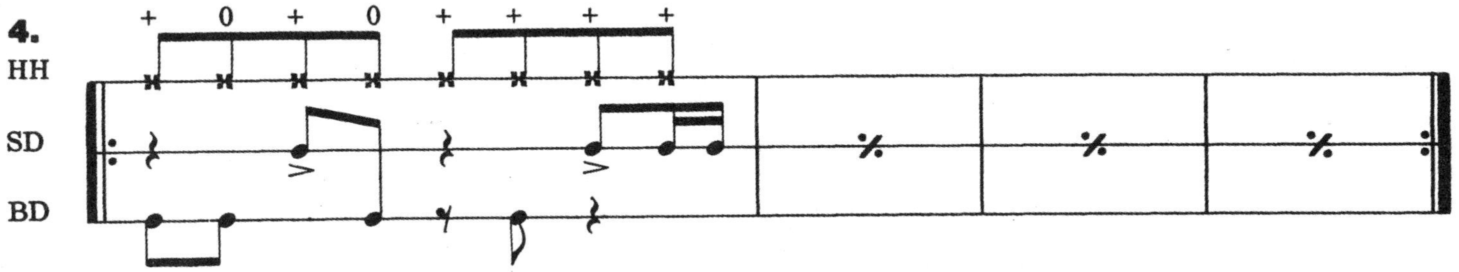

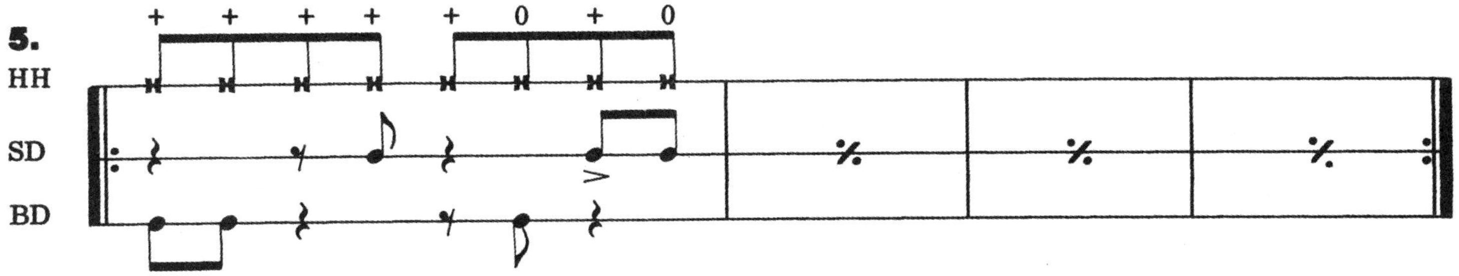

1.
+ + + + + + + 0
HH
SD
BD

2.
+ + + 0 + 0 + 0
HH
SD
BD

3.
+ + + 0 + + + 0
HH
SD
BD

4.
+ 0 + 0 + + + +
HH
SD
BD

5.
+ + + + + 0 + 0
HH
SD
BD

Sixteen Bar Exercise (Eighth Notes)

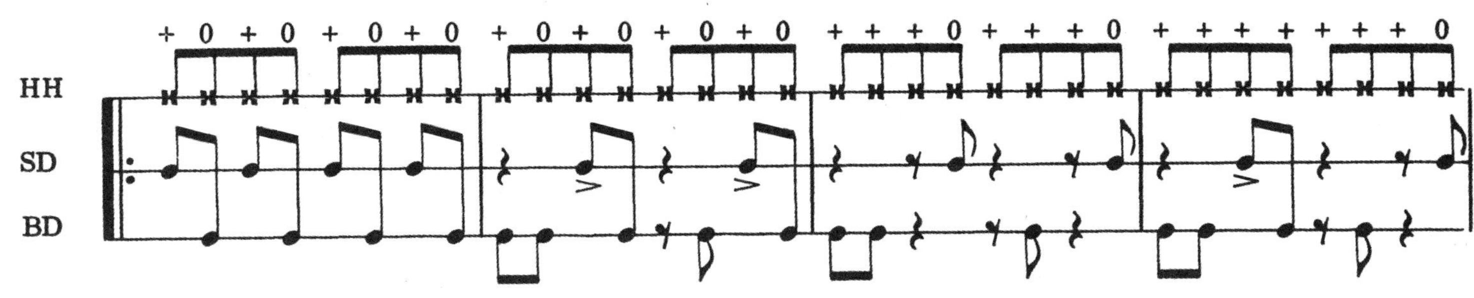

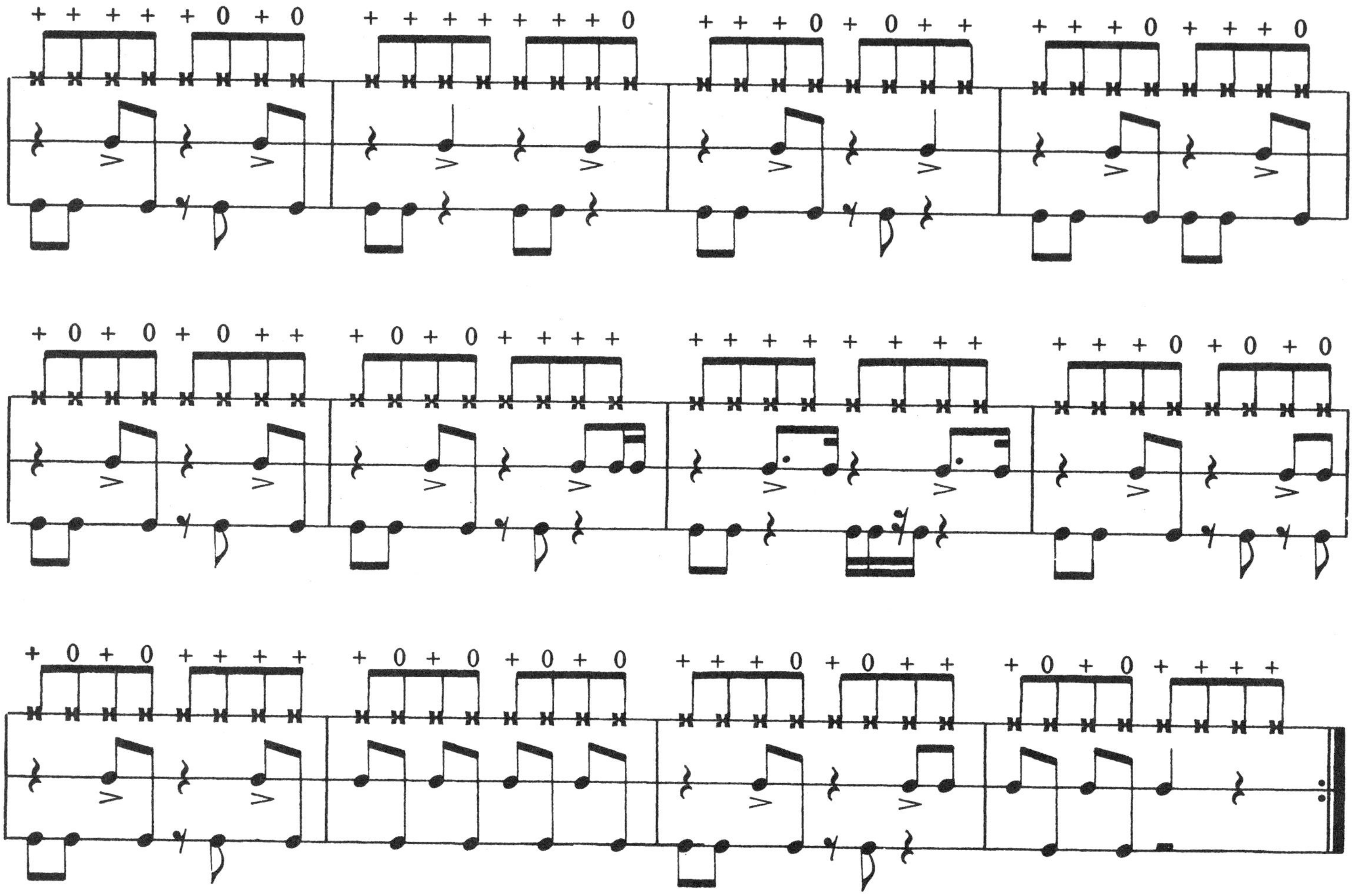

Sixteenth Note Hi-Hat Rhythms

Play HH sixteenths on closed Hi-Hat Cymbals.

1.

2.

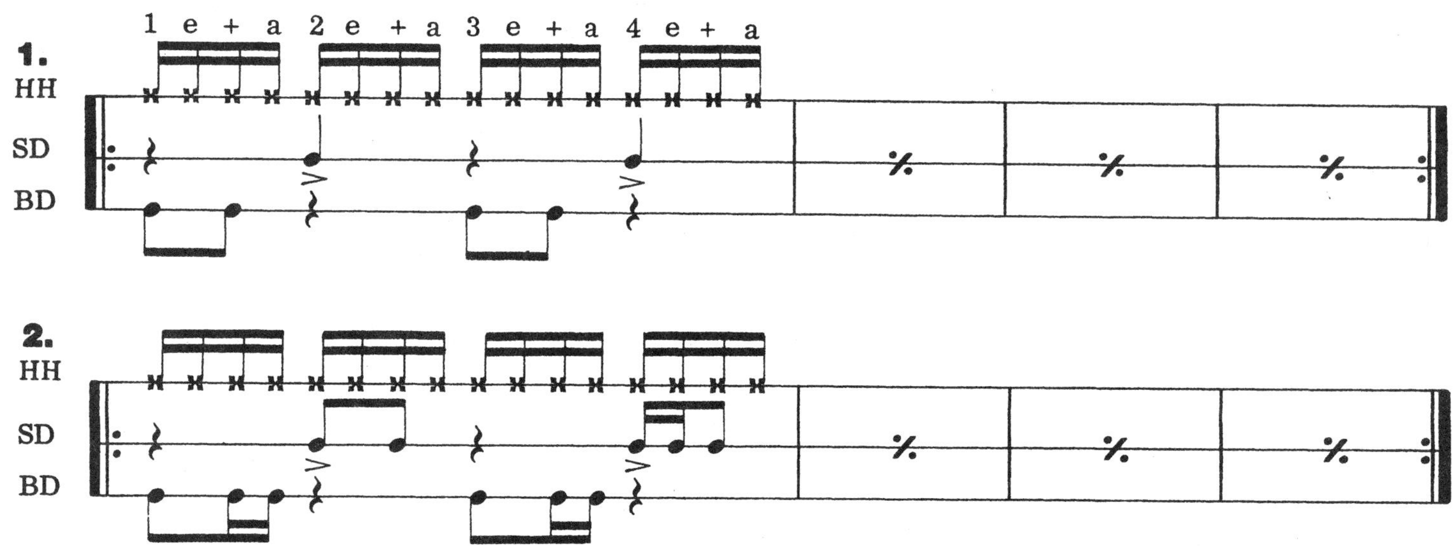

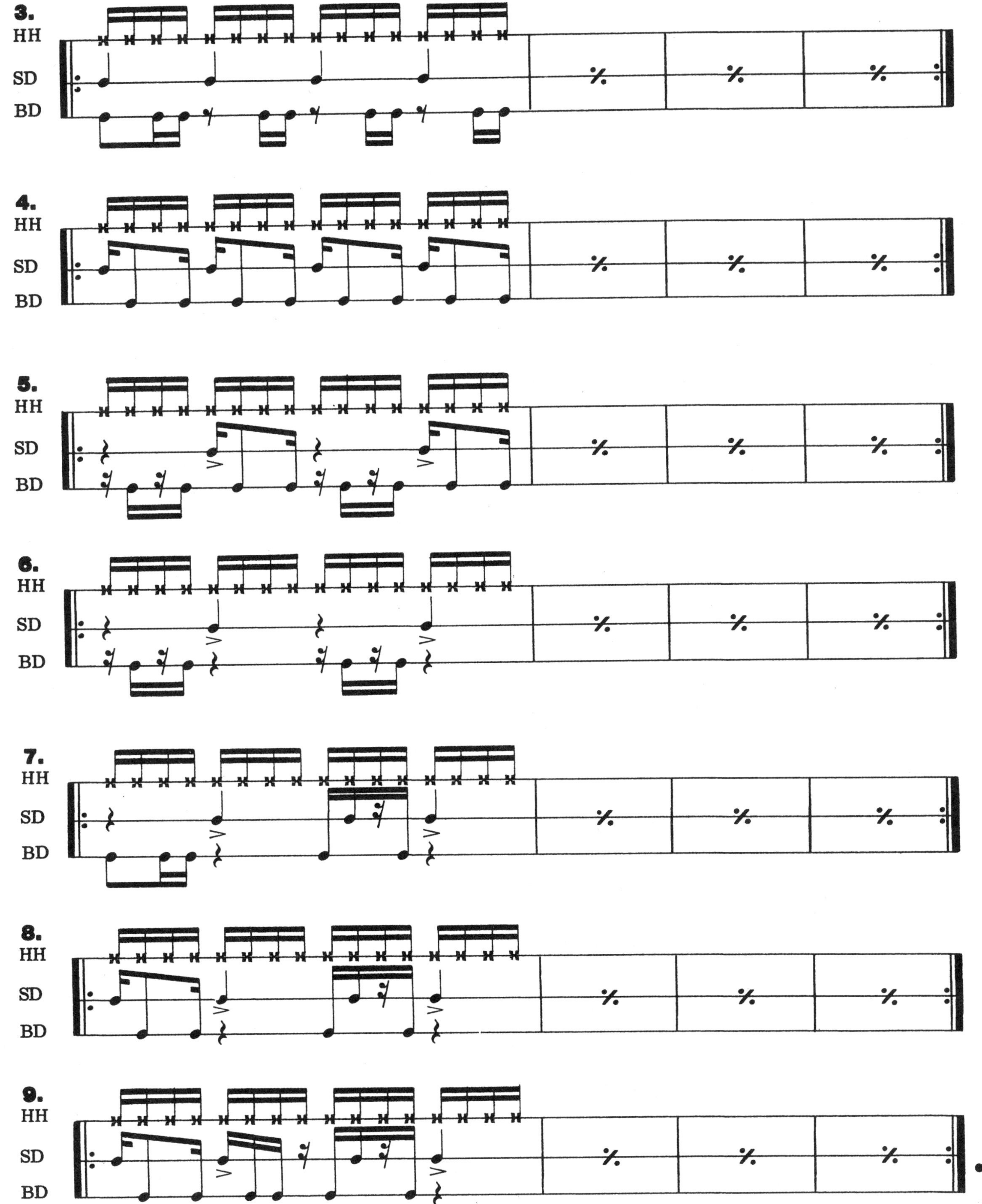
3.
HH
SD
BD
4.
HH
SD
BD
5.
HH
SD
BD
6.
HH
SD
BD
7.
HH
SD
BD
8.
HH
SD
BD
9.
HH
SD
BD

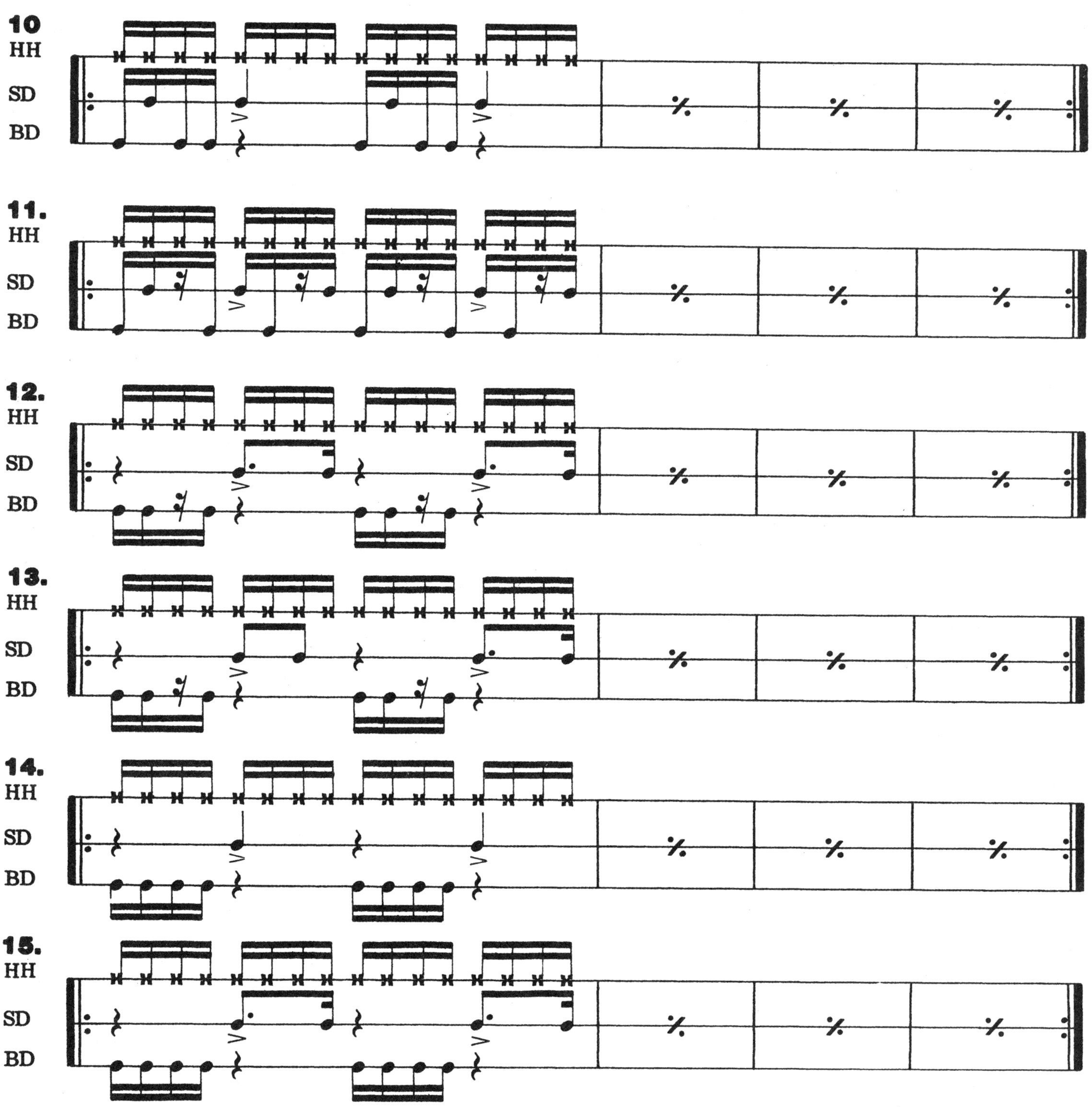
10
HH
SD
BD
11.
HH
SD
BD
12.
HH
SD
BD
13.
HH
SD
BD
14.
HH
SD
BD
15.
HH
SD
BD

Sixteen Bar Exercise (Sixteenth Notes)

Play HH sixteenths on closed Hi-Hat Cymbals

Sixteenth Notes — Accented — Open And Closed

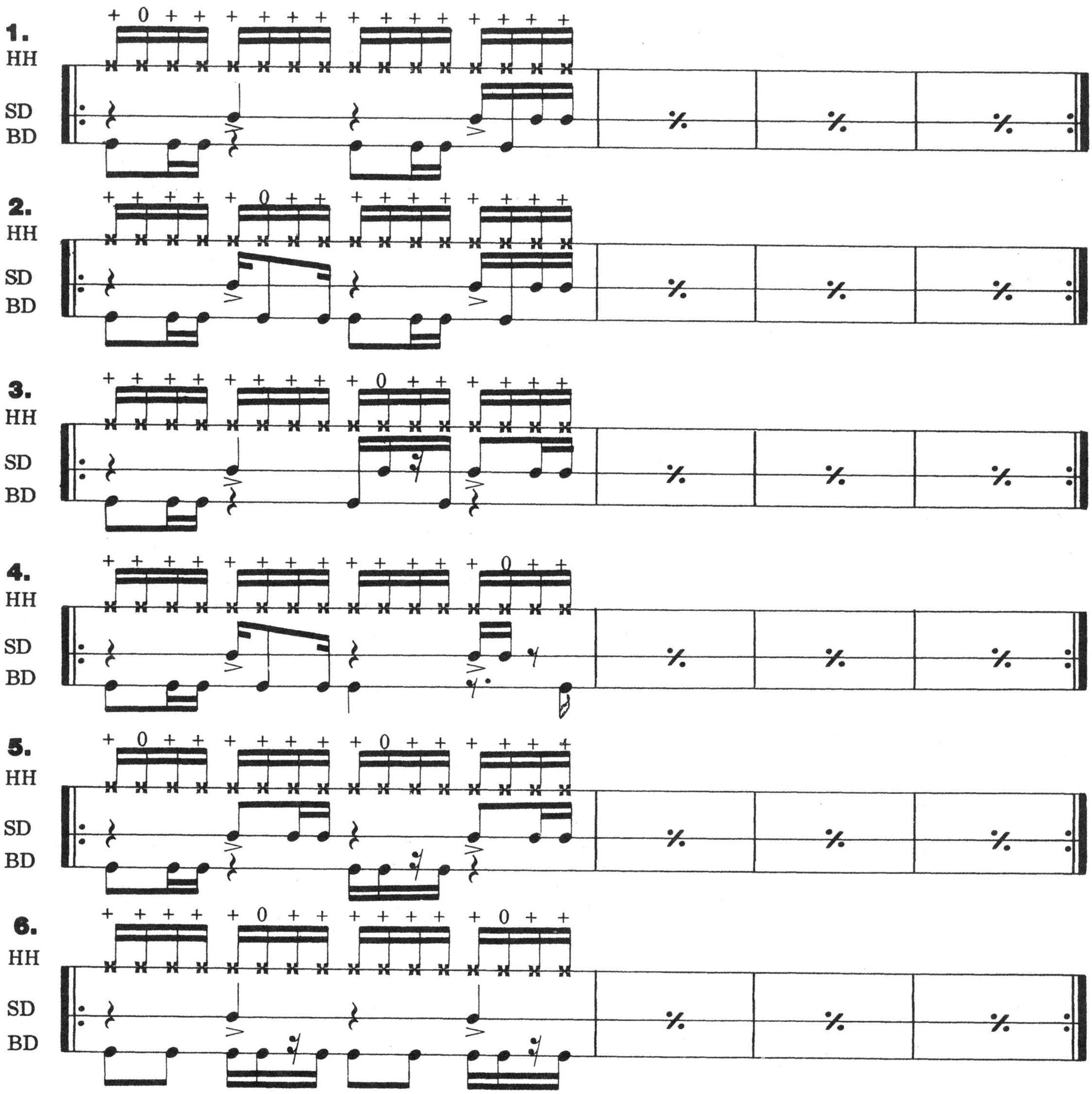

1.
+ 0 + + + + + + + + + + + + + +
HH
SD
BD

2.
+ + + + + 0 + + + + + + + + + +
HH
SD
BD

3.
+ + + + + + + + + 0 + + + + + +
HH
SD
BD

4.
+ + + + + + + + + + + + + 0 + +
HH
SD
BD

5.
+ 0 + + + + + + + 0 + + + + + +
HH
SD
BD

6.
+ + + + + 0 + + + + + + + 0 + +
HH
SD
BD

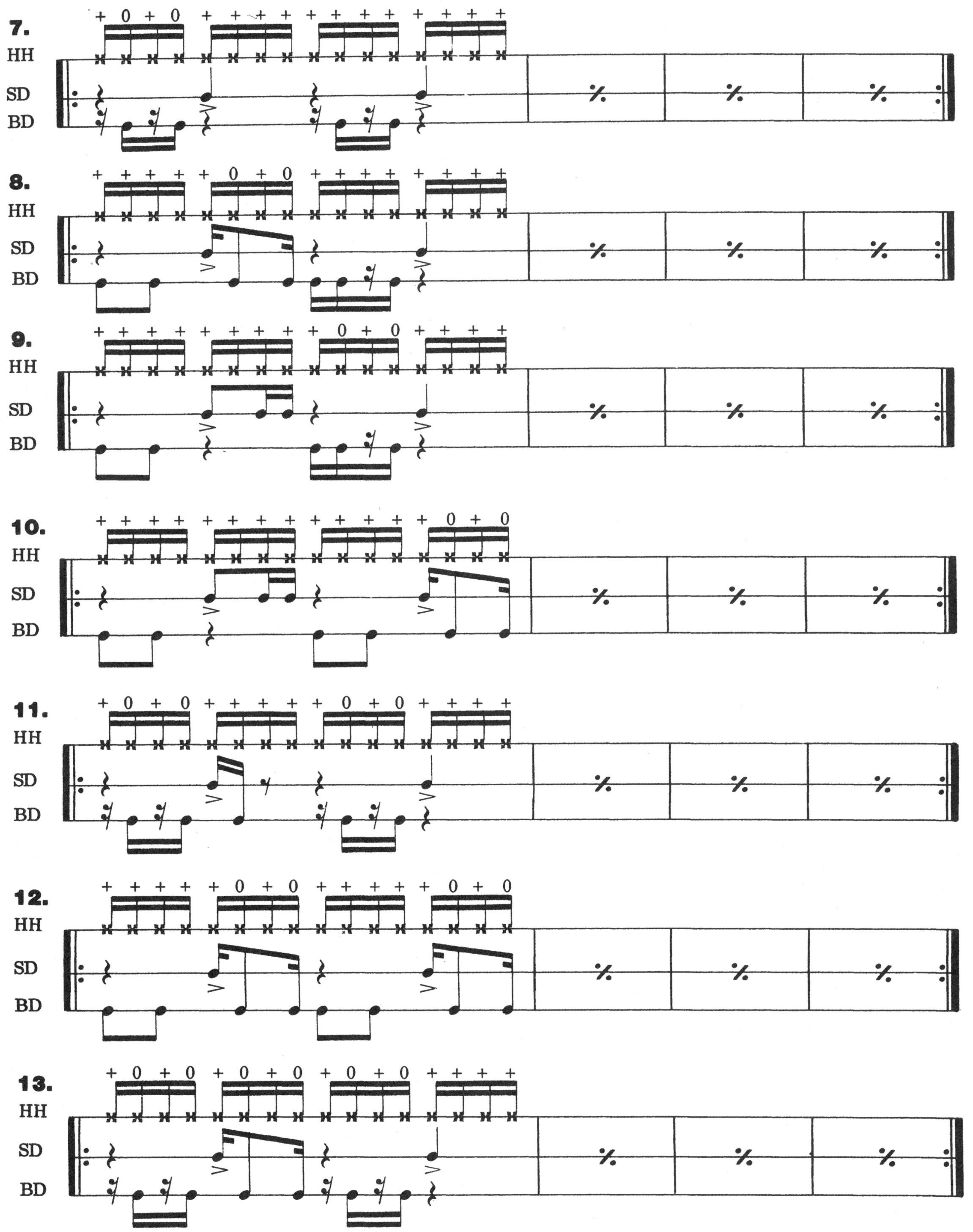
7.
HH
SD
BD
8.
HH
SD
BD
9.
HH
SD
BD
10.
HH
SD
BD
11.
HH
SD
BD
12.
HH
SD
BD
13.
HH
SD
BD

14.

15.

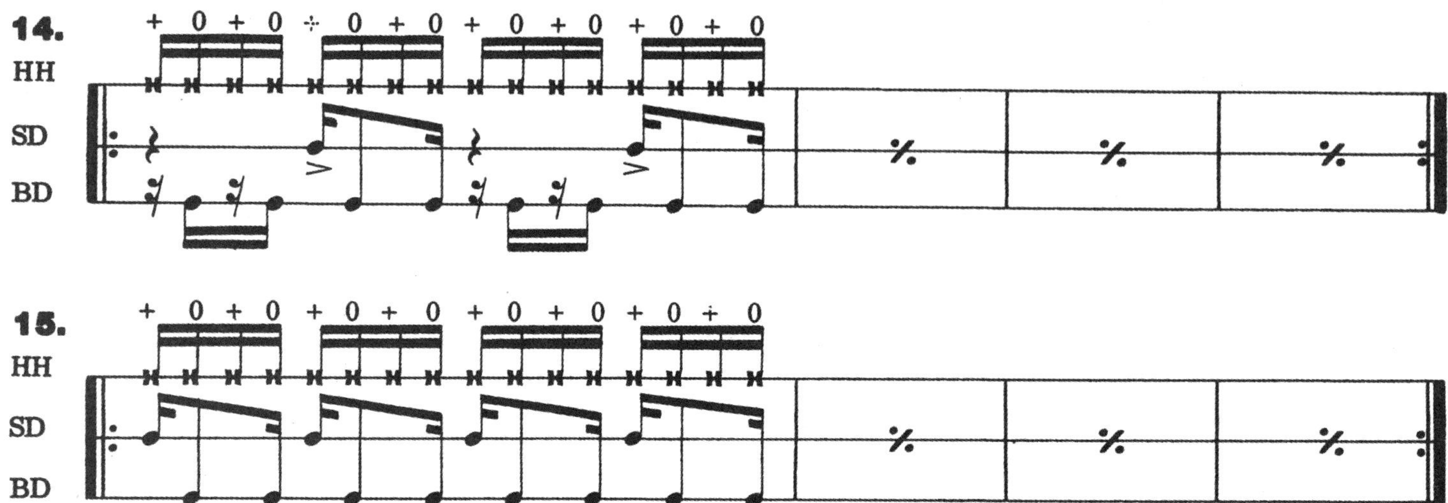

12 Bar Exercise

The following is a twelve bar exercise of accented sixteenth notes with the Hi-Hat opening and closing. The accent occurs when the cymbals are played in the open position.

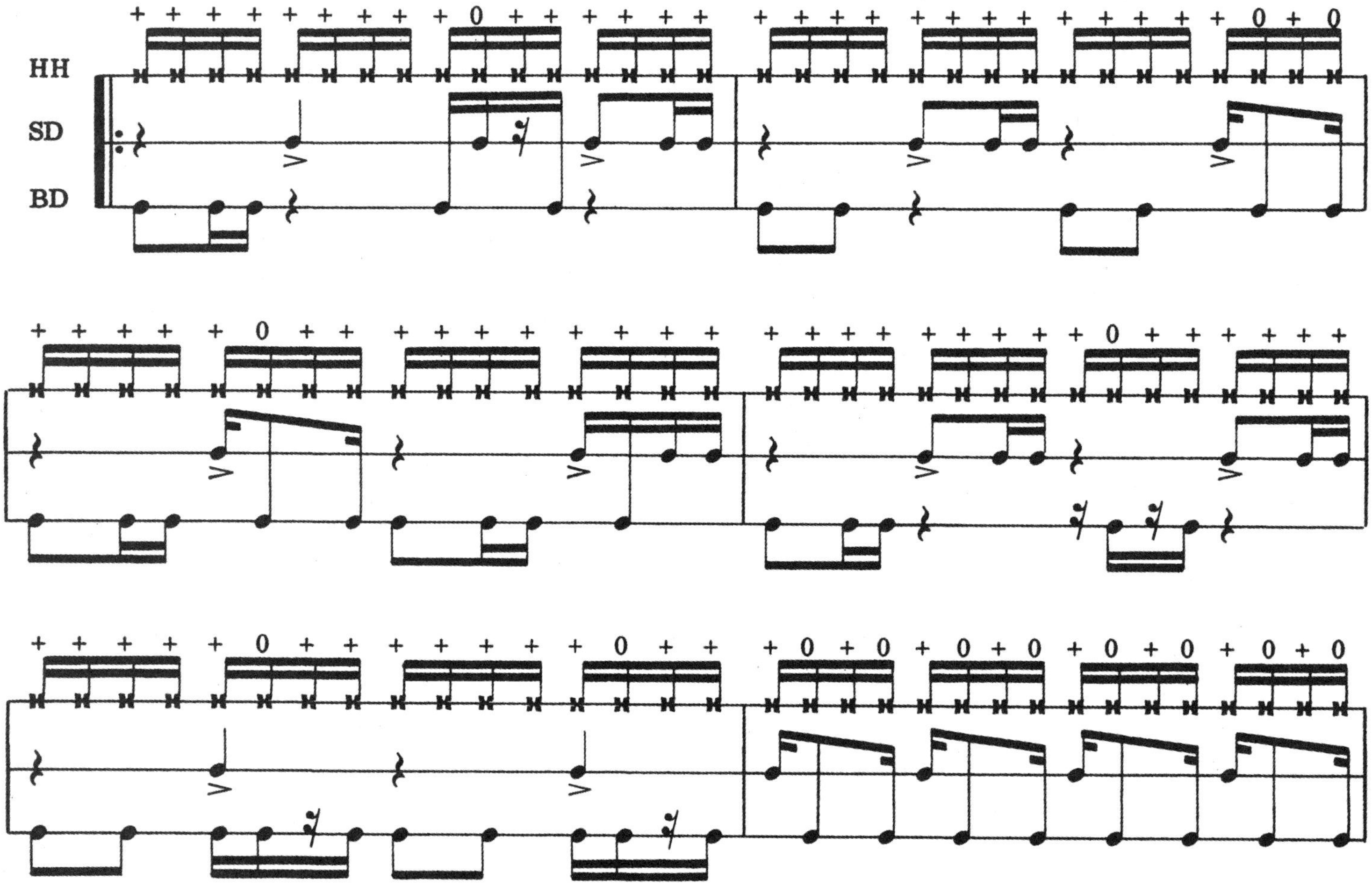

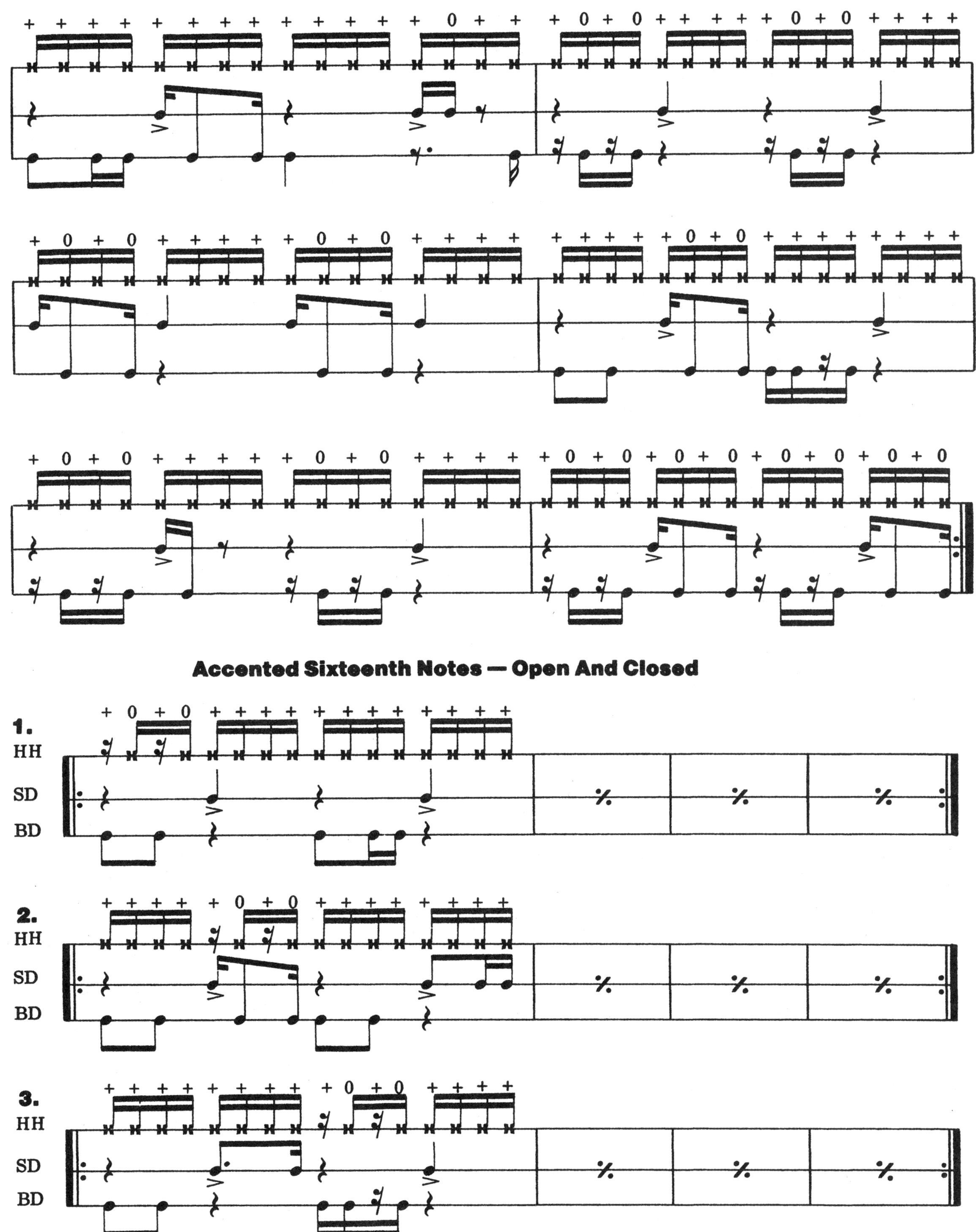
Accented Sixteenth Notes — Open And Closed
1.
HH
SD
BD
2.
HH
SD
BD
3.
HH
SD
BD

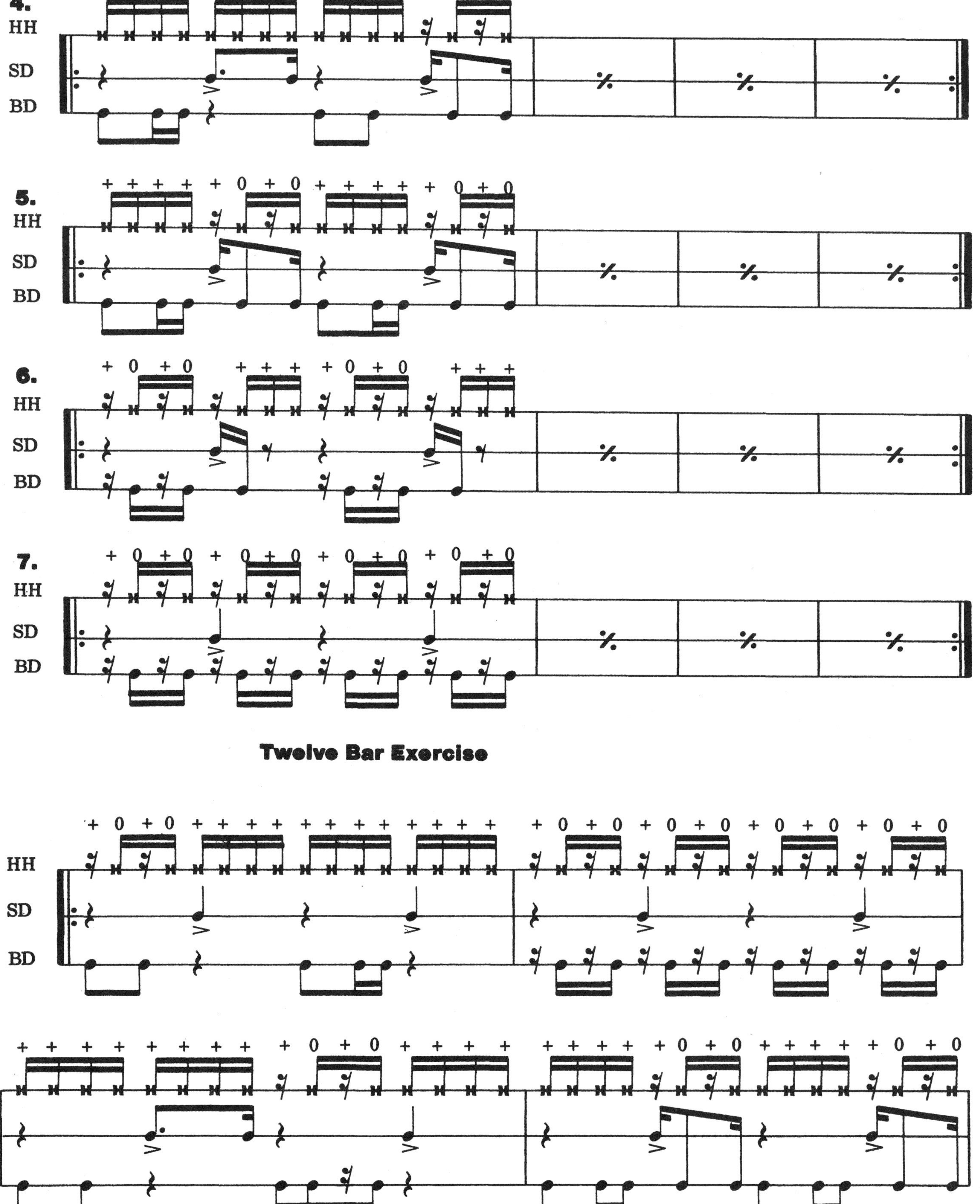

Twelve Bar Exercise

Advanced Sixteenth Note Rhythms

Audio

Exercises 1-5 are played on the HH and SD using alternate stickings.

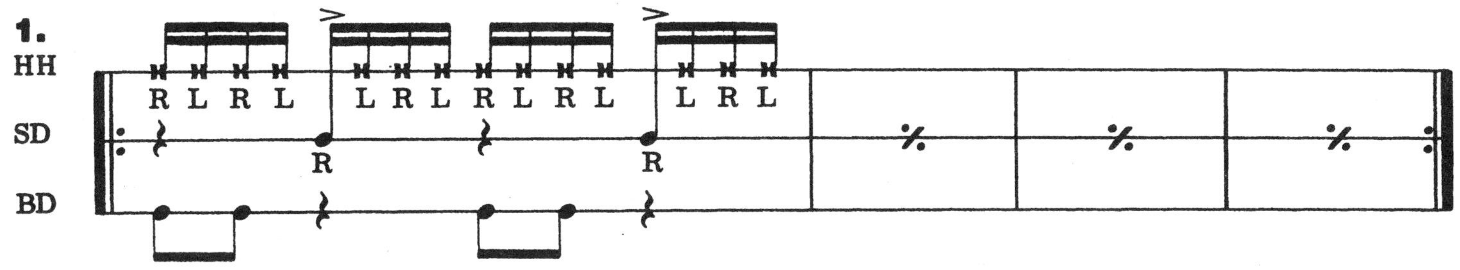

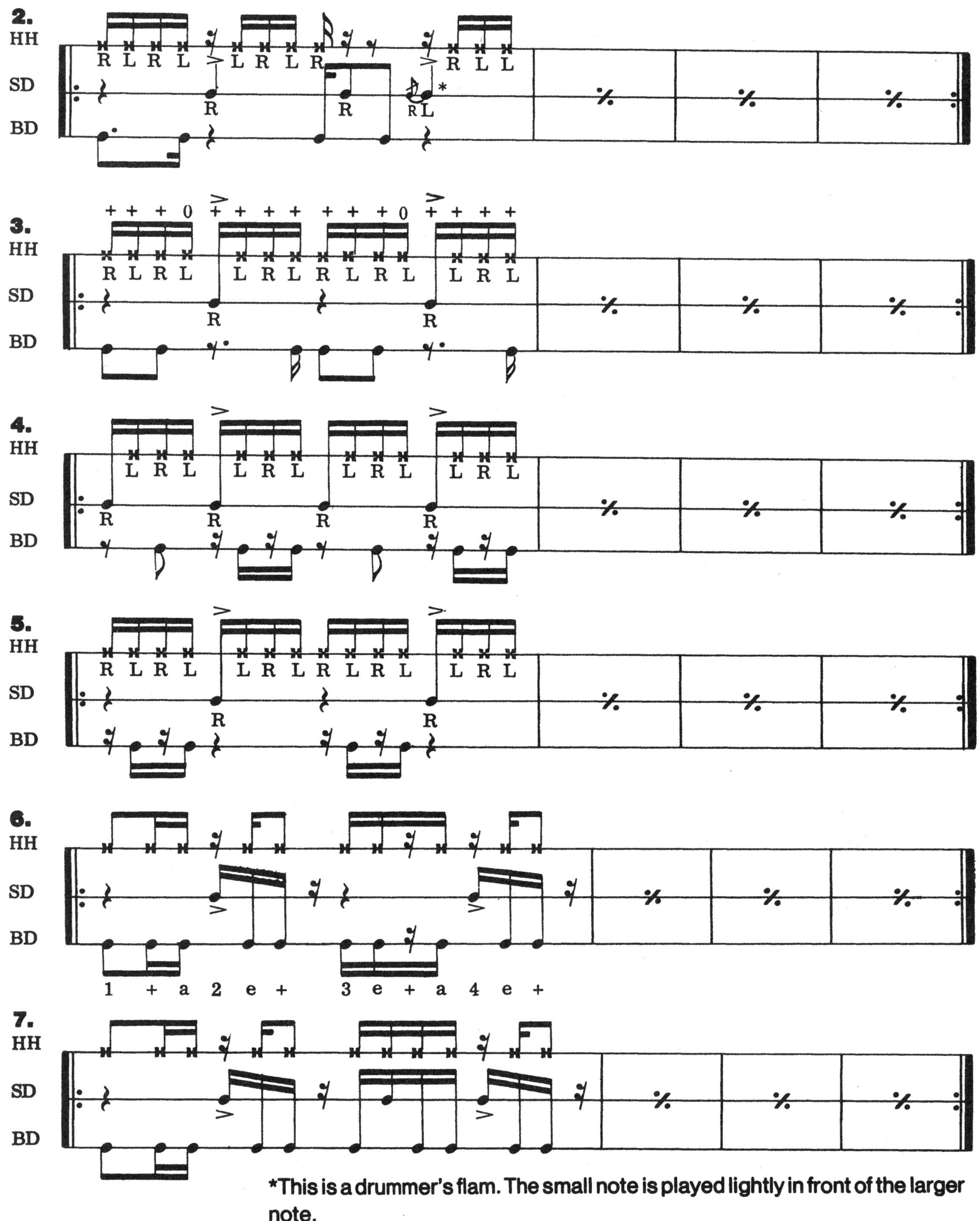

*This is a drummer's flam. The small note is played lightly in front of the larger note.

8.
HH
SD
BD
Eight Bar Exercise
HH
SD
BD
R L R L L R L R L R L L R L R L R L L R L R L R L L R L
R R R R
L R L L R L L R L L R L
R R R R
R L R L L R L R L R L R L R L R L R L R L R L R
R R R R R R

Rock Poly-Rhythms

In these exercises the right foot plays the same pattern as the right hand!

Right hand on cymbal or Hi-Hat (x)
Left hand on snare drum (♩)
(Left-handed drummers should reverse the sticking.)

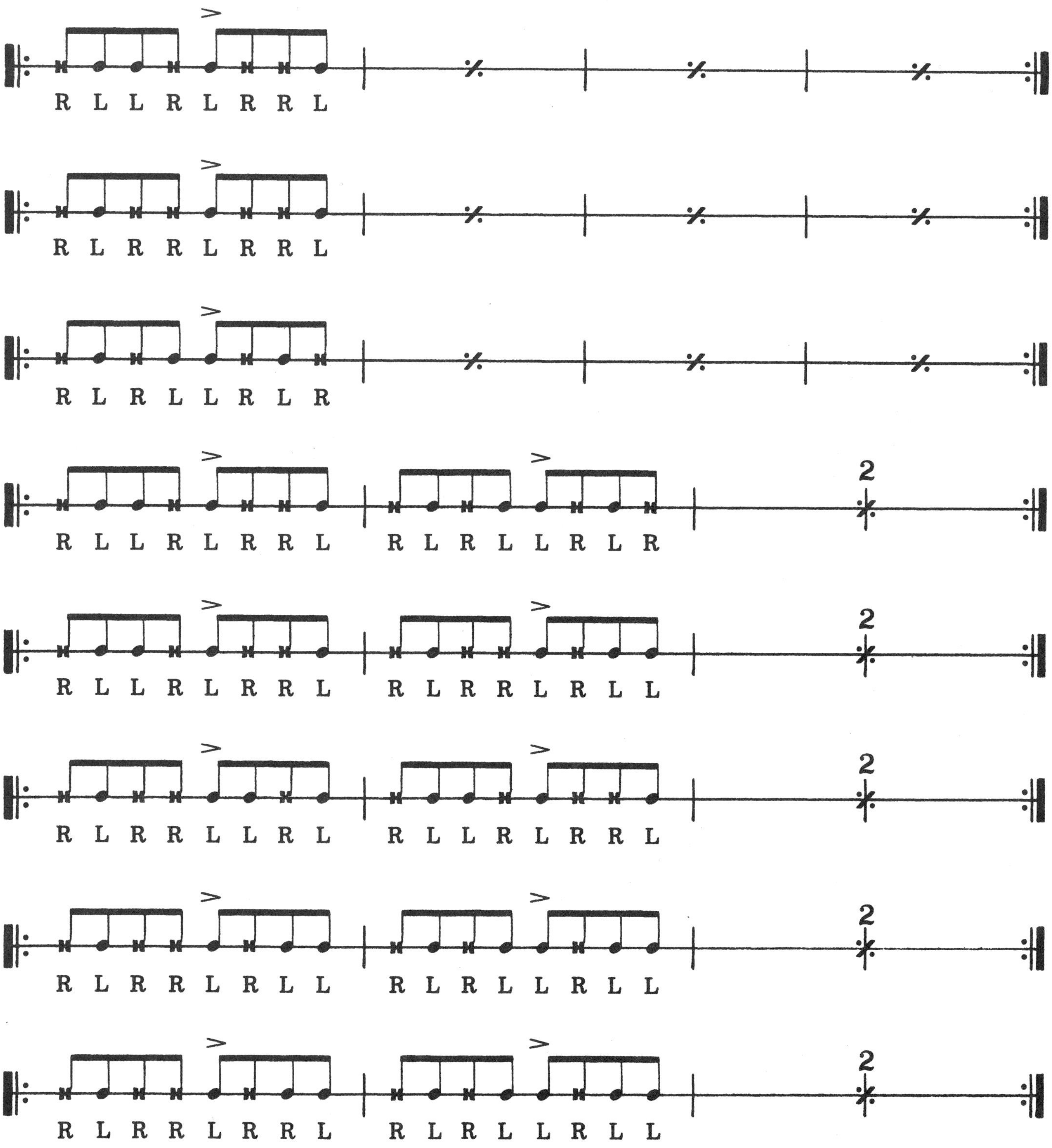

R L L R L R R L

R L R R L R R L

R L R L L R L R

R L L R L R R L   R L R L L R L R

R L L R L R R L   R L R R L R L L

R L R R L L R L   R L L R L R R L

R L R R L R L L   R L R L L R L L

R L R R L R R L   R L R L L R L L

Part 9

Review

All the rhythms in parts II-VIII are covered in this review.

These exercises can be played as professional rock solos in 14 or 16 bar breaks. The cymbal line can be played on either the ride cymbal (RC) or Hi-Hat cymbals (HH) except where specifically noted for HH (+/o).

HH
RC
SD
BD

+ 0 + 0 + 0 + 0 + 0 + 0 + 0 + 0
R R

Sixteen Bar Solo 2.

Sixteen Bar Solo 3.
HH
RC
SD
BD

Sixteen Bar Solo 4.
HH
RC
SD
BD

+ 0 + 0
R R
+ 0 + 0 + + + + + 0 + 0 + + + +
+ 0 + + + + + + + + + + + + + +
+ + + + + 0 + 0 + + + + + + + +
+ + + + + + + 0
+ + + + + + + 0

Part 10

Shuffle Rhythms (Bounce)

To create a bounce feeling, the shuffle rhythm uses dotted eighth and sixteenth notes between hands and feet. Quarter notes are played on the cymbal, instead of the usual eighths. The natural emphasis is on 2 and 4.

Dotted Eighths And Sixteenths

1. HH RC SD BD

2. HH RC SD BD

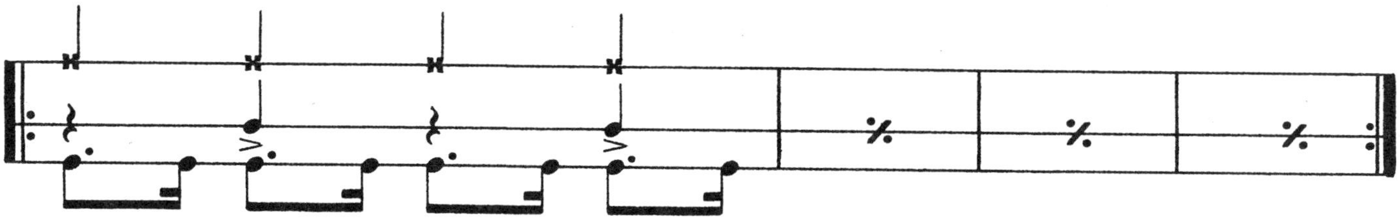

3. HH RC SD BD

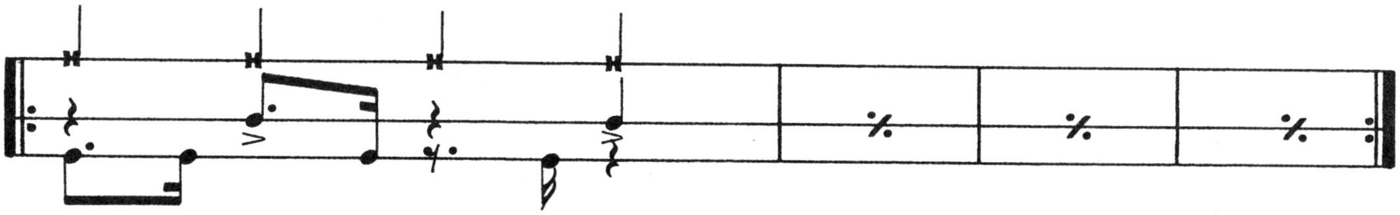

4. HH RC SD BD

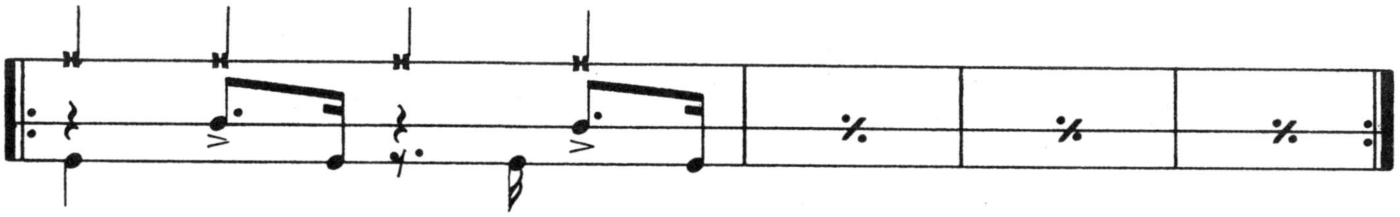

5. HH RC SD BD

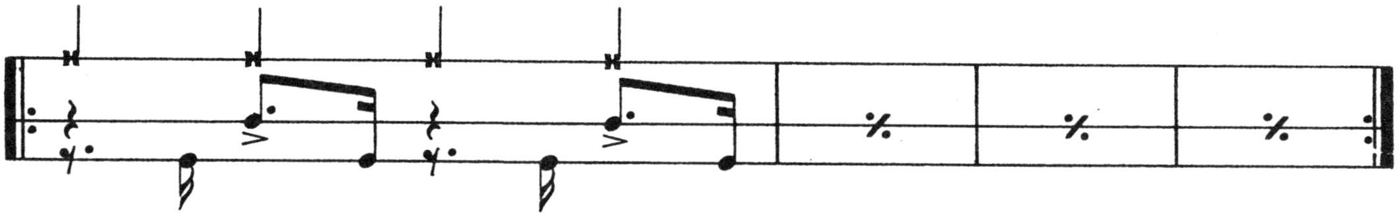

6. HH RC SD BD

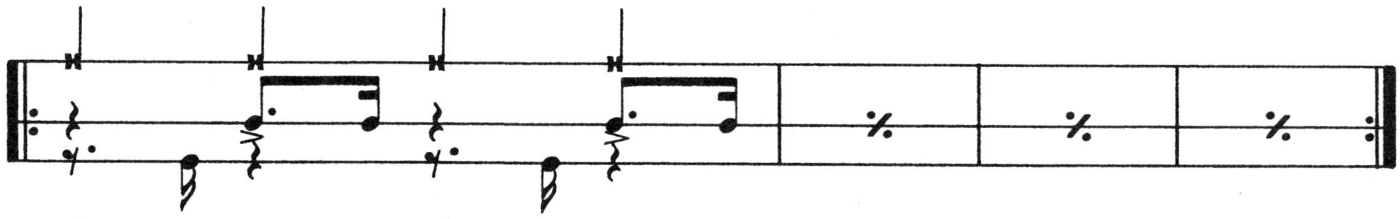

7. HH RC SD BD

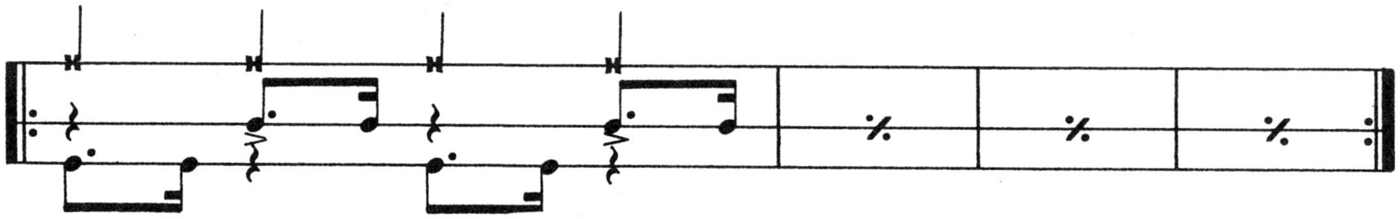

8.
HH
RC
SD
BD

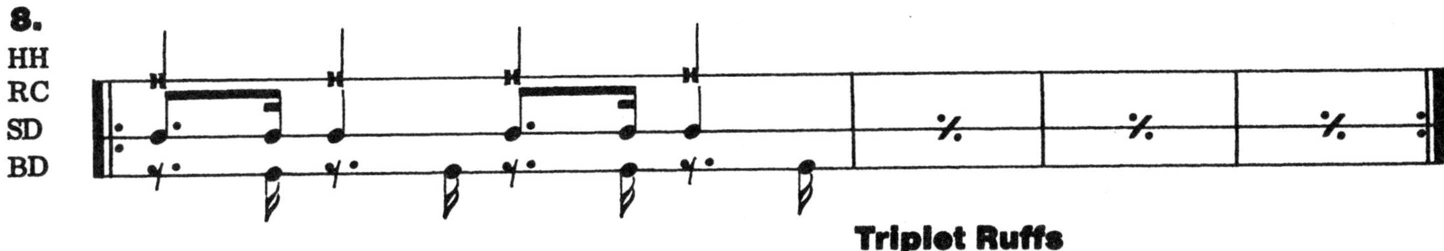

Triplet Ruffs

The sixteenth note triplets on this page are part of an embellishment known to drummers as a "ruff." In the following exercises, triplets are played against quarter notes on the cymbal. In this section, eighth note triplets are counted:

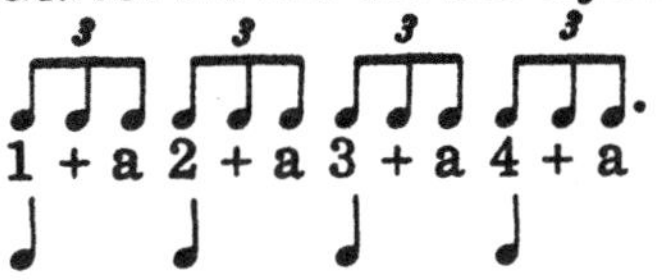
1 + a 2 + a 3 + a 4 + a

1.
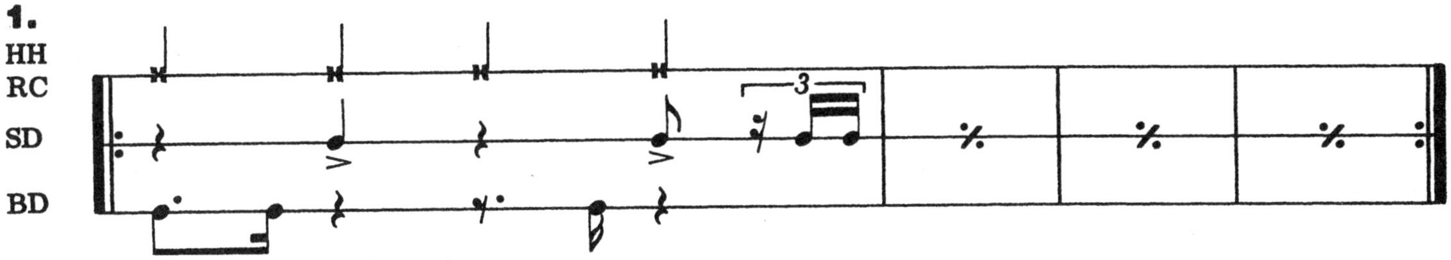
HH
RC
SD
BD

2.
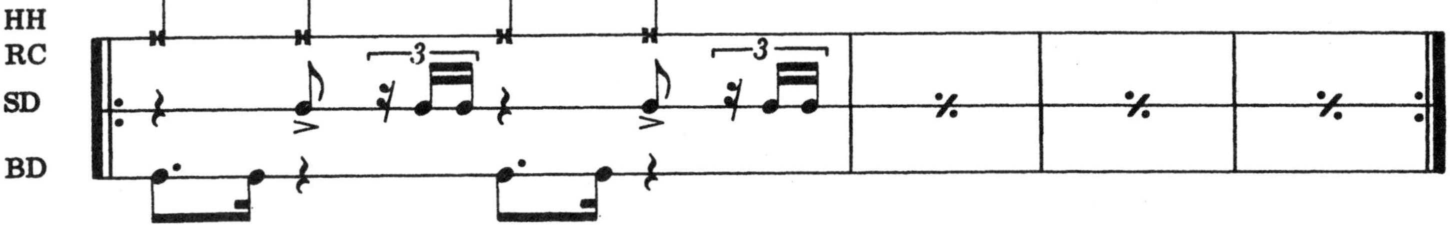
HH
RC
SD
BD

3.
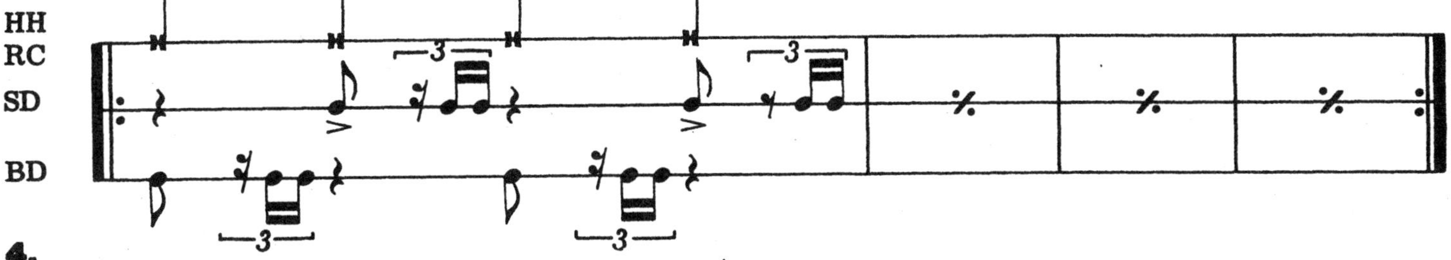
HH
RC
SD
BD

4.
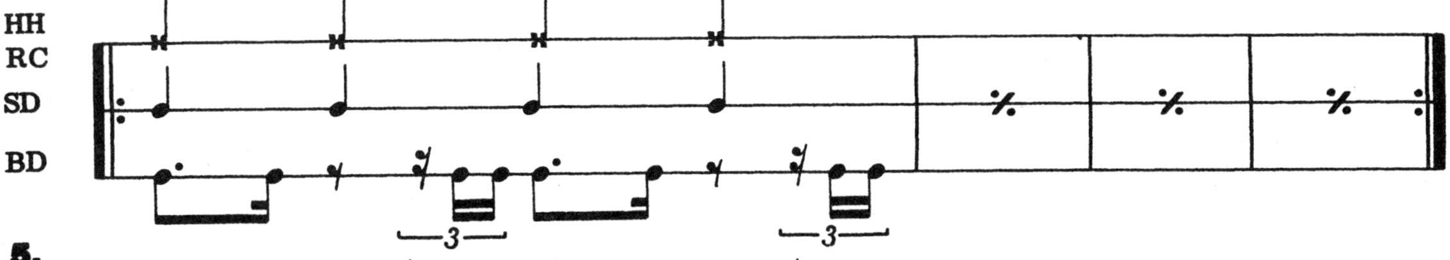
HH
RC
SD
BD

5.
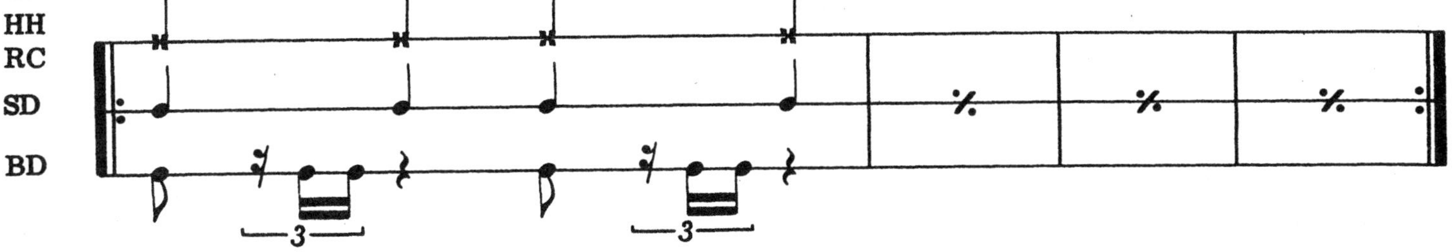
HH
RC
SD
BD

Eighth Note Triplets For Bass Drum

8.
HH
RC
SD
BD
3
3
3
3
Sixteen Bar Exercise
HH
RC
SD
BD
3
3
3
3
3
3
3
3
3
3

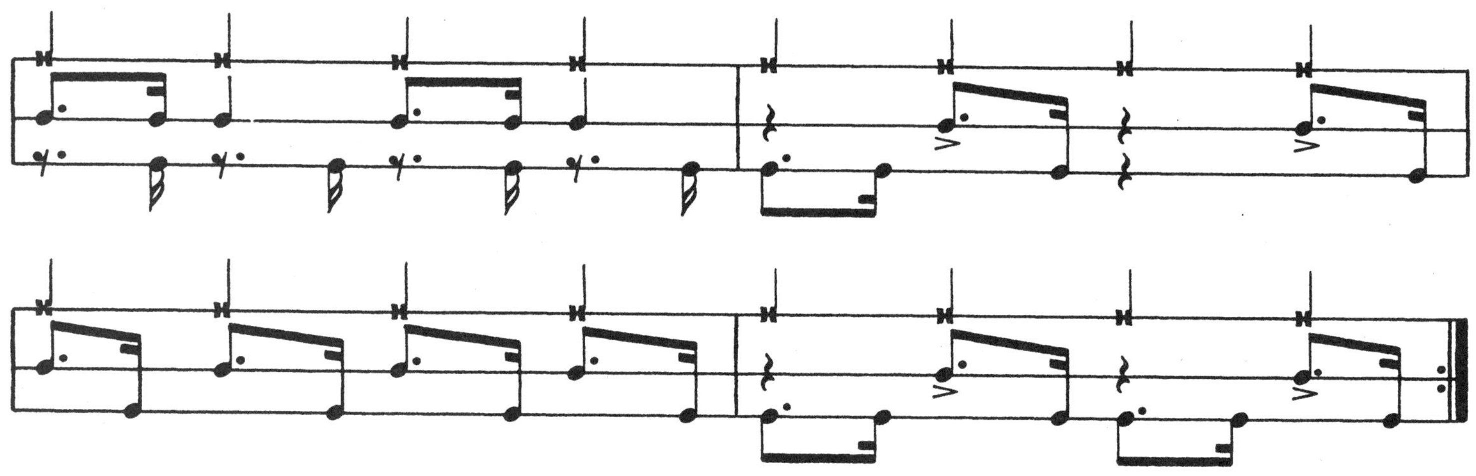

Shuffle Rhythms

These shuffle rhythms are played with dotted eighth and sixteeenth notes, rather than quarter notes, on cymbal. Improvising occurs between the snare and bass drum.

Dotted Eighth and Sixteenth On Top

Improvising on Snare and Bass Drum

1.
HH
RC
SD
BD

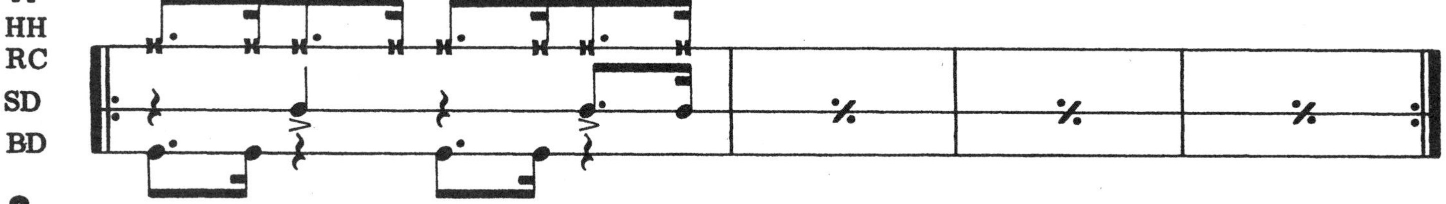

2.
HH
RC
SD
BD

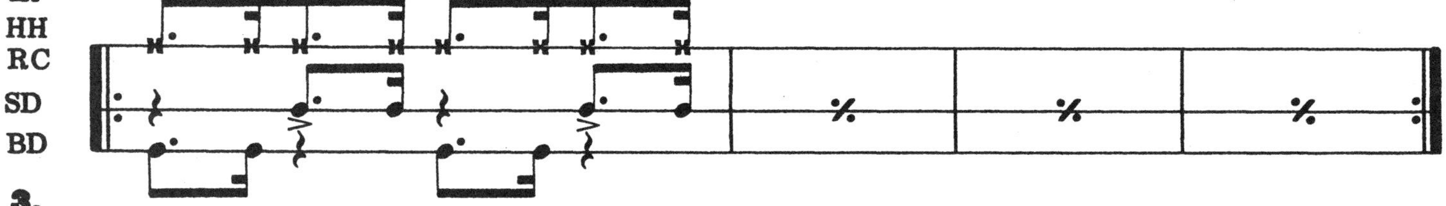

3.
HH
RC
SD
BD

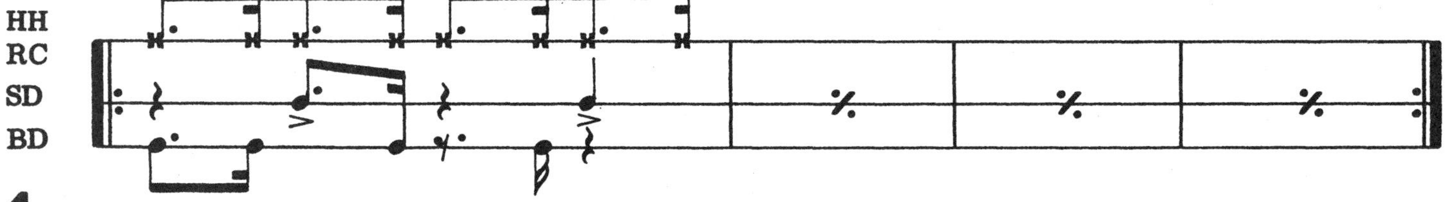

4.
HH
RC
SD
BD

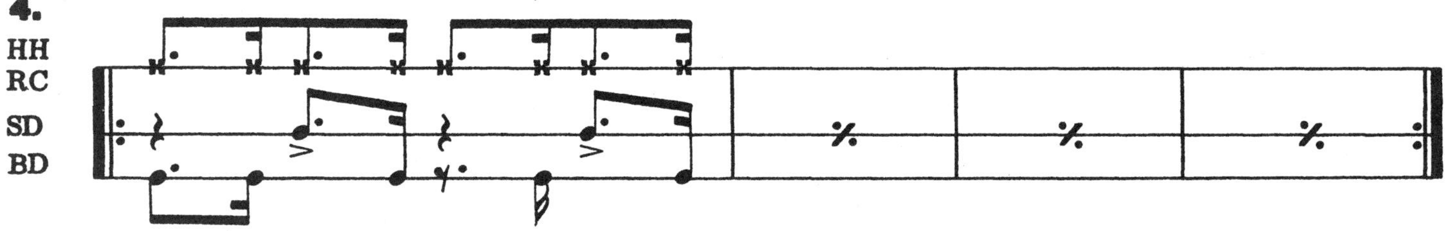

5.
HH
RC
SD
BD

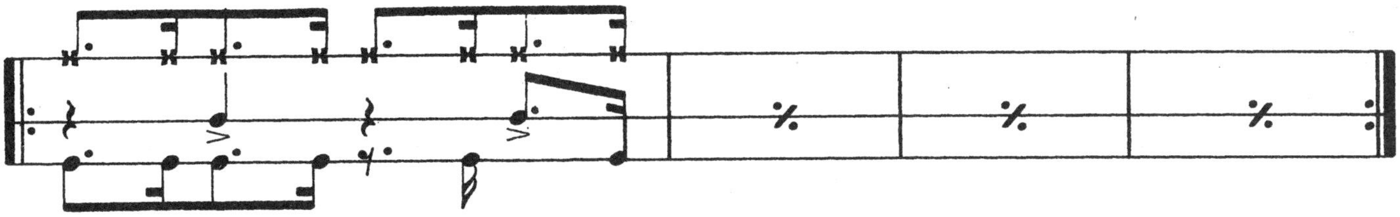

6.
HH
RC
SD
BD

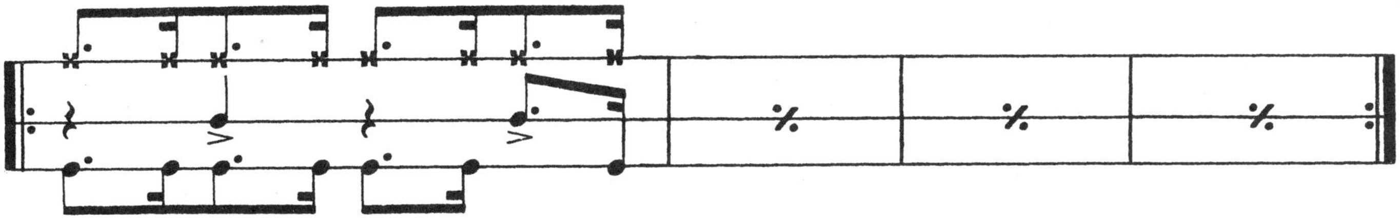

7.
HH
RC
SD
BD

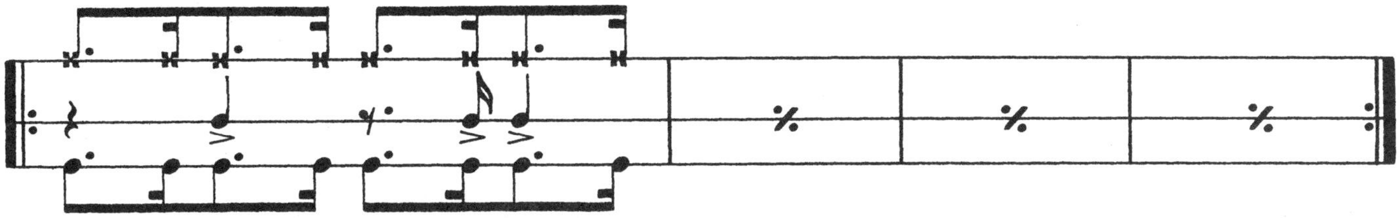

8.
HH
RC
SD
BD

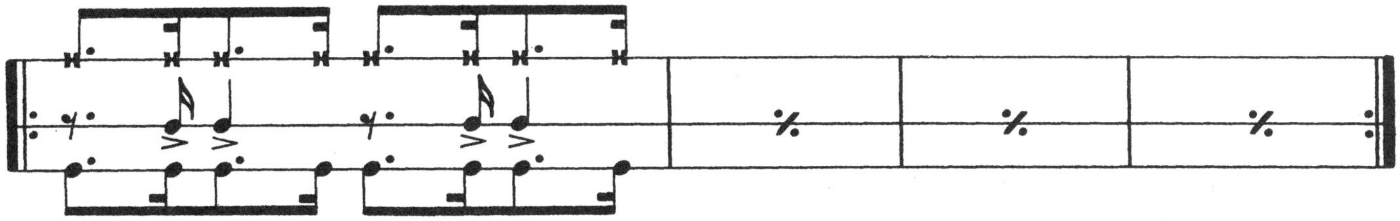

Eight Bar Exercise

Dotted Eighth And Sixteenth Notes

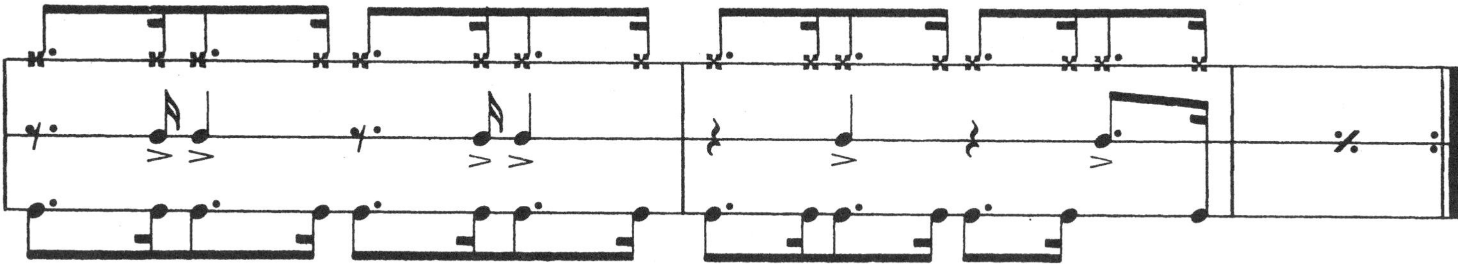

Part 11

Rock Fills

Here are a number of fills that I use. They can be easily adapted for any playing situation. The drums are marked at the beginning of each line as follows:

RC	Ride Cymbal
ST	Small Tom-Tom
SD	Snare Drum
LT	Large Tom-Tom
BD	Bass Drum

Sticking choice is dependent upon physical set-up and musical inflection.

Stickings which have worked well for me are indicated with R and L.

One Bar Breaks

The first measure is the fill. The second measure shows the standard rhythm that might come before and after the fill.

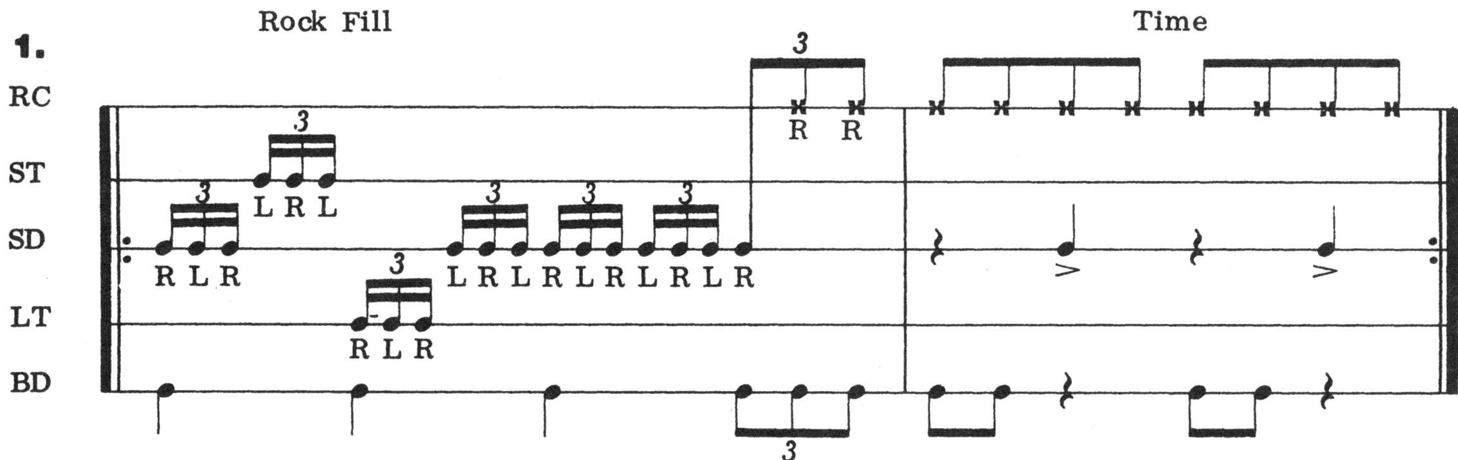

2.
RC
ST
SD
LT
BD
L R L R L R L R L
R
R L
L
3.
RC
ST
SD
LT
BD
R R L
R R
L R L R
L R L L
R
4.
RC
ST
SD
LT
BD
R L
R L
R L
R L
5.
RC
ST
SD
LT
BD
3
LL R L R L R L
R L R L
R L

6.

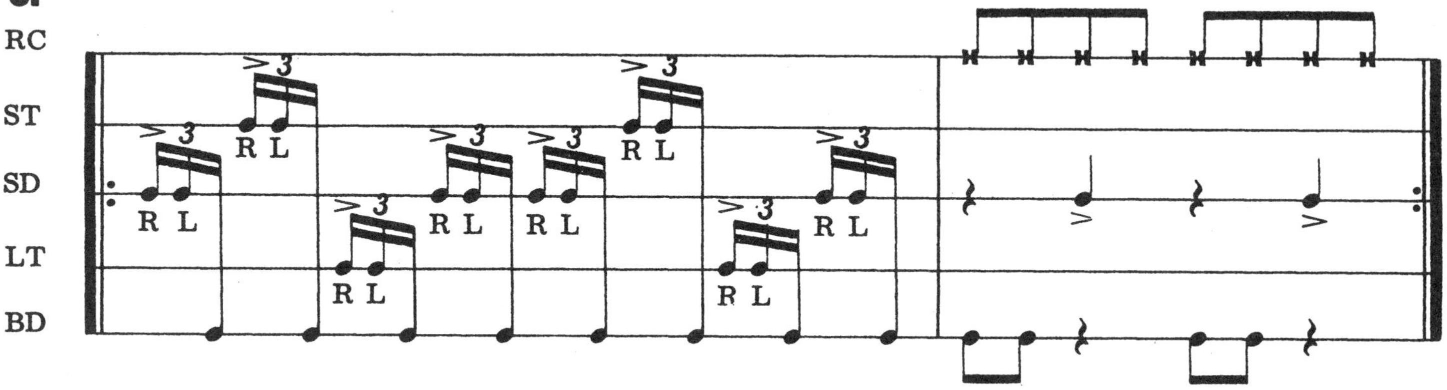

RC
ST
SD
LT
BD

7.

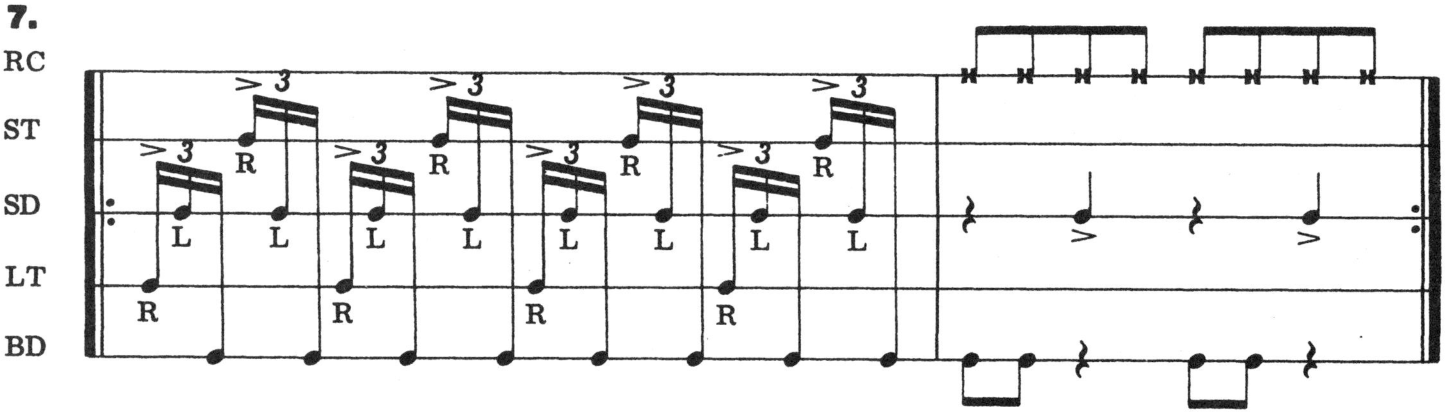

RC
ST
SD
LT
BD

Two Bar Breaks

The first two measures are the fill.

1.

Rock Fill
Time
RC
ST
SD
LT
BD

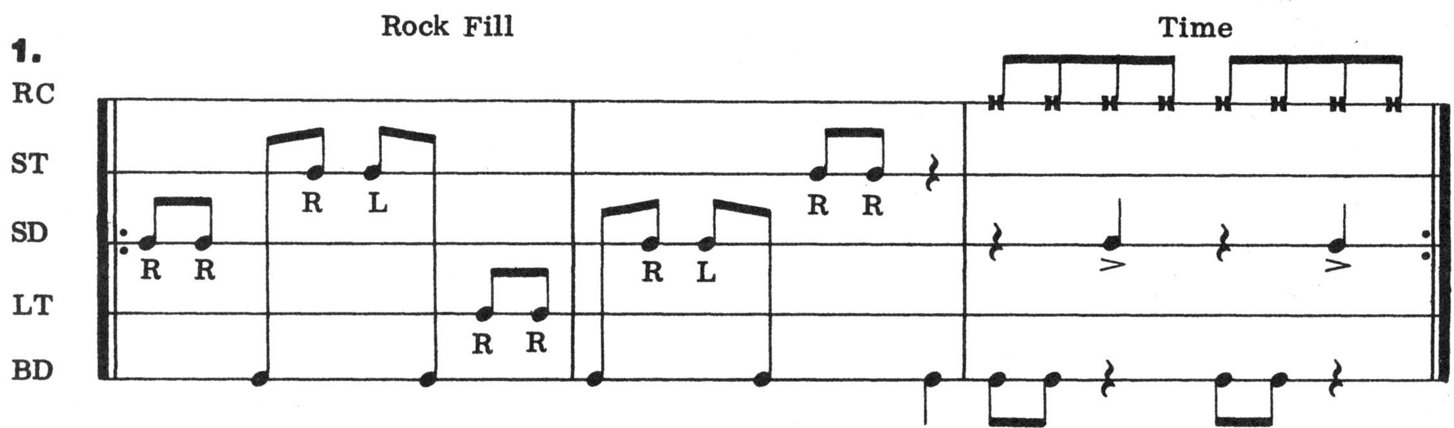

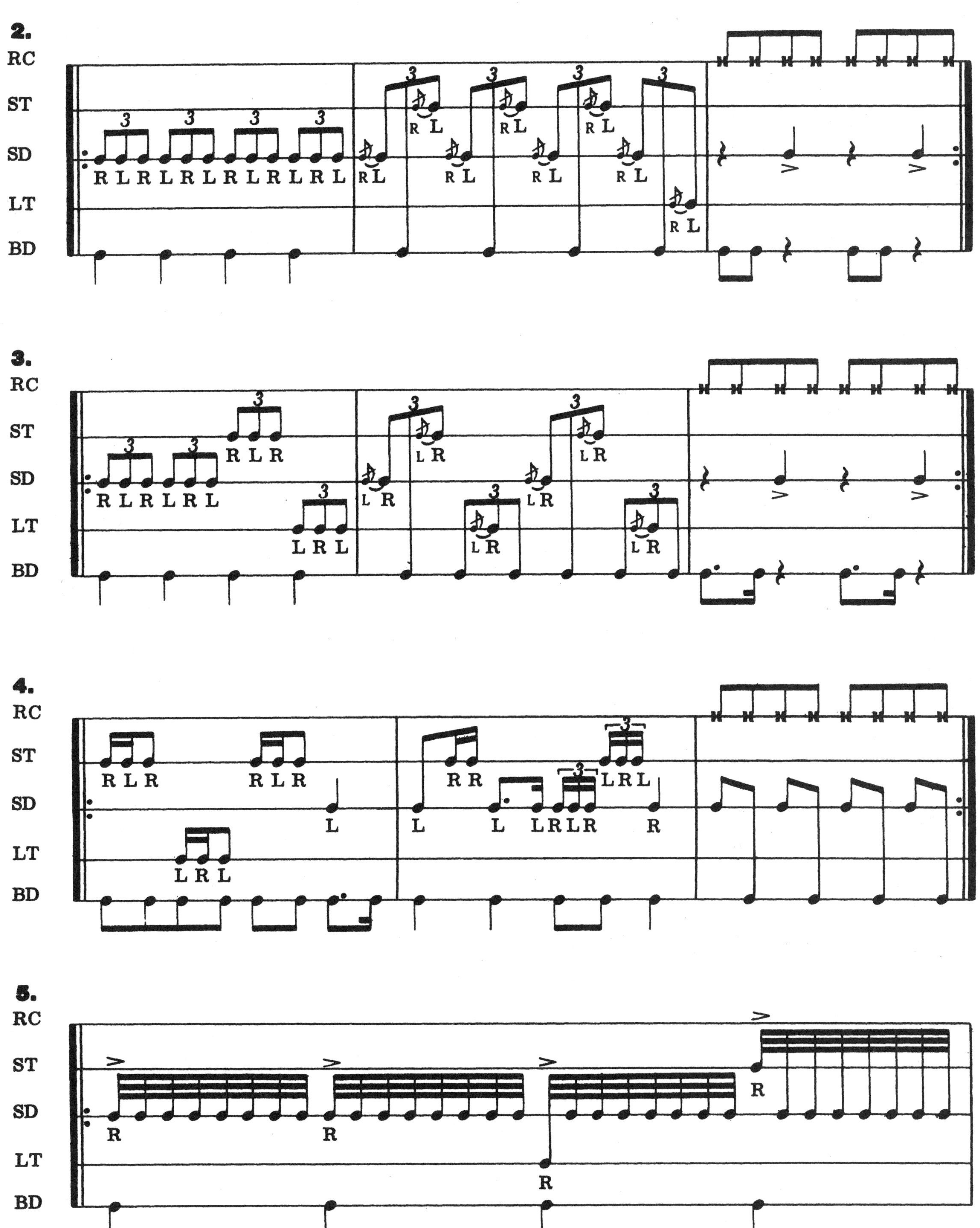
2.
RC
ST
SD
LT
BD
R L R L R L R L R L R L
R L
R L
R L
R L
R L
R L
R L
R L
3.
RC
ST
SD
LT
BD
R L R L R L
R L R
L R L
L R
L R
L R
L R
L R
L R
4.
RC
ST
SD
LT
BD
R L R
R L R
L
L R L
L
R R
L
L R L R
L R L
R
5.
RC
ST
SD
LT
BD
R
R
R
R

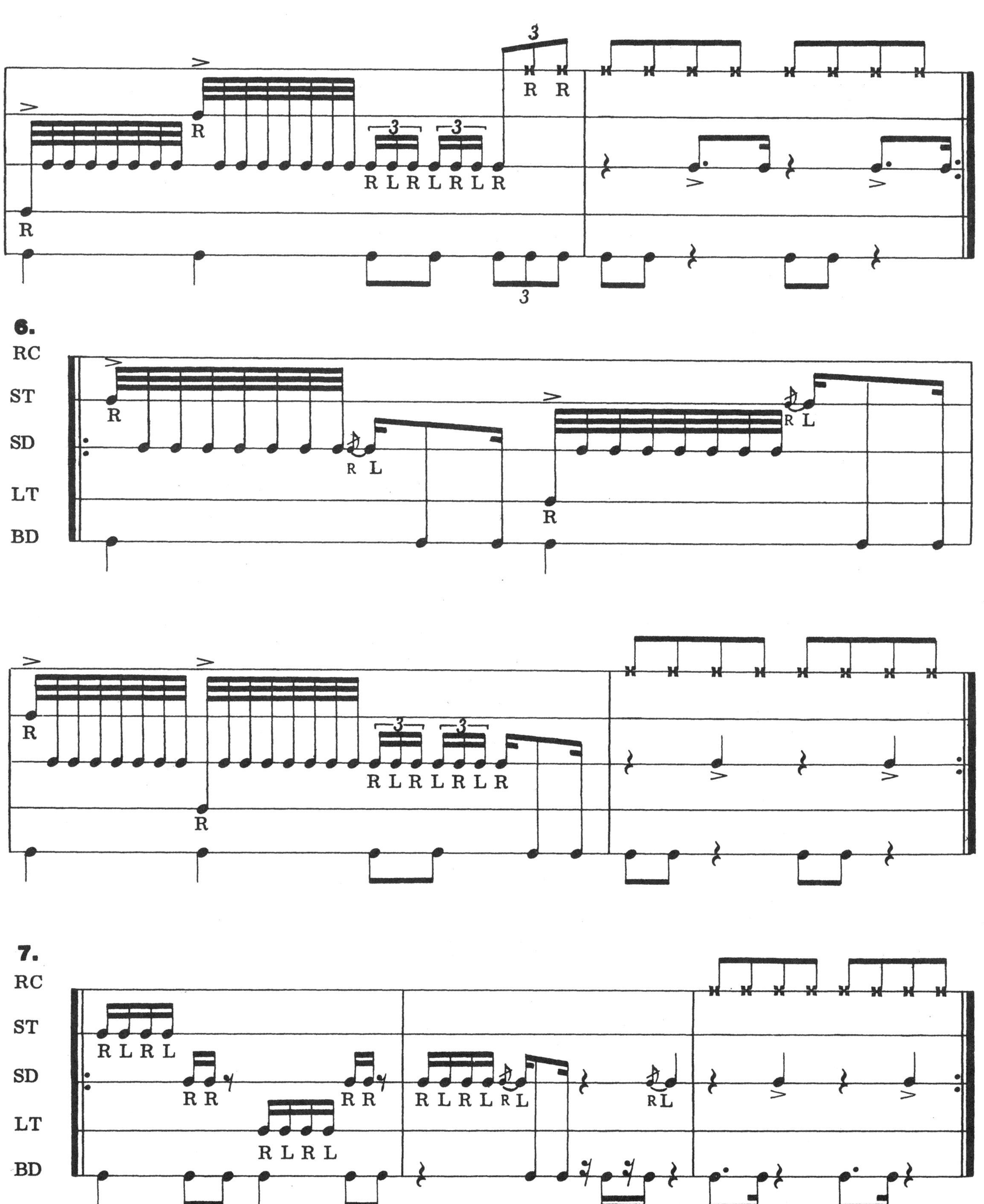

6.
RC
ST
SD
LT
BD
7.
RC
ST
SD
LT
BD

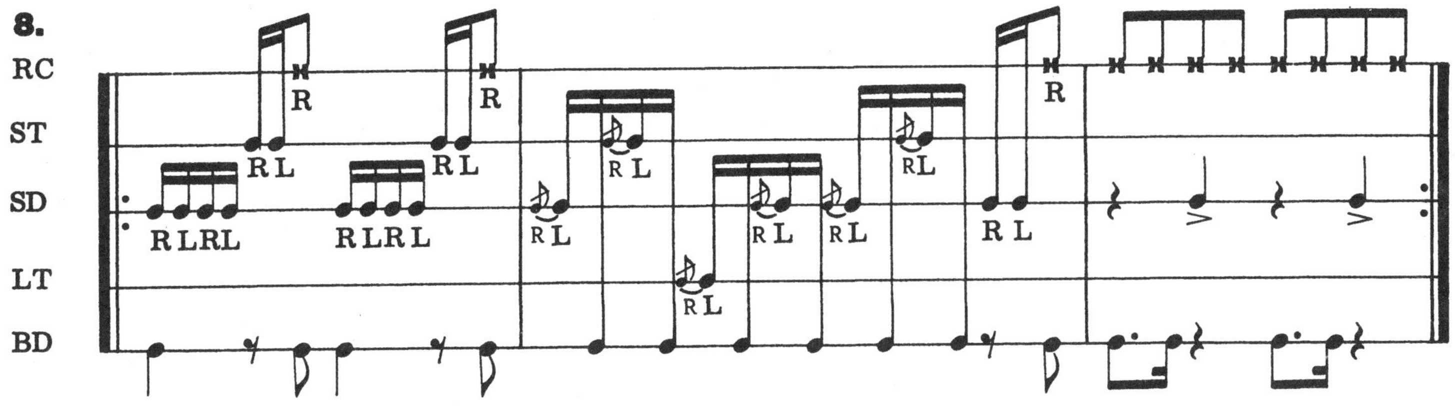

Part 12

Double Bass

Double bass drumming is not as hard as it looks—it's just like adding another line to the music.

Example

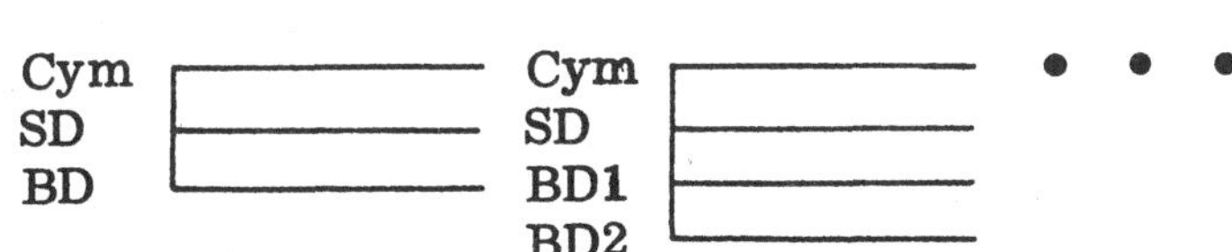

Use the ride cymbal as indicated. BD1 is the main bass drum (right for right handed drummers, left for left handed drummers) and BD2 is the second bass drum. Look at relationships. Figure out the rhythms. Take it slow!

Using Quarter Notes on BD2

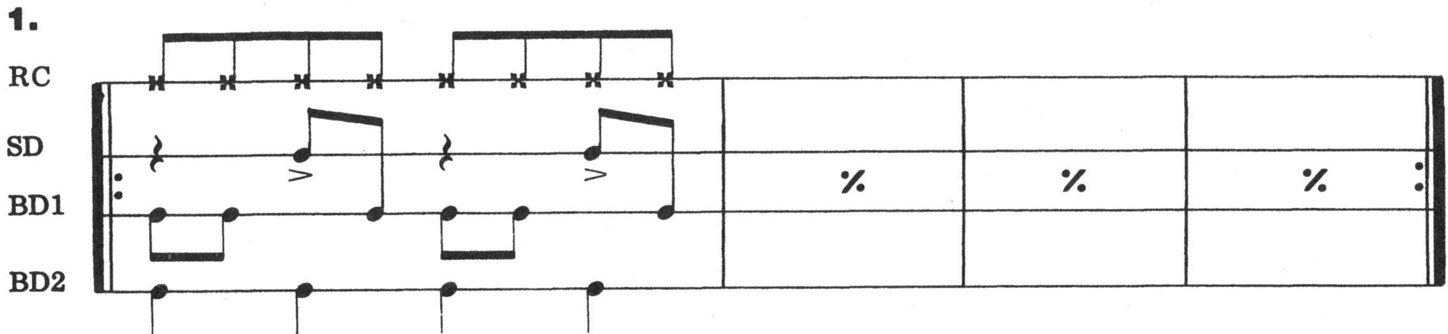

2.

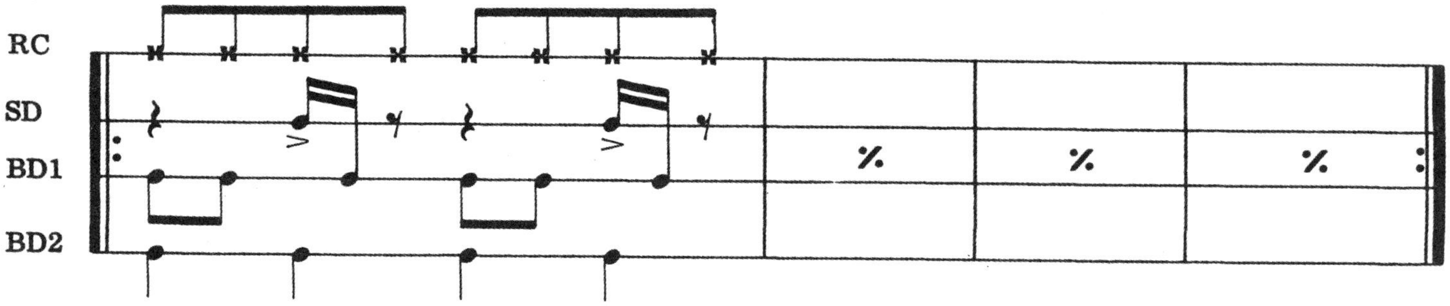

RC
SD
BD1
BD2

3.

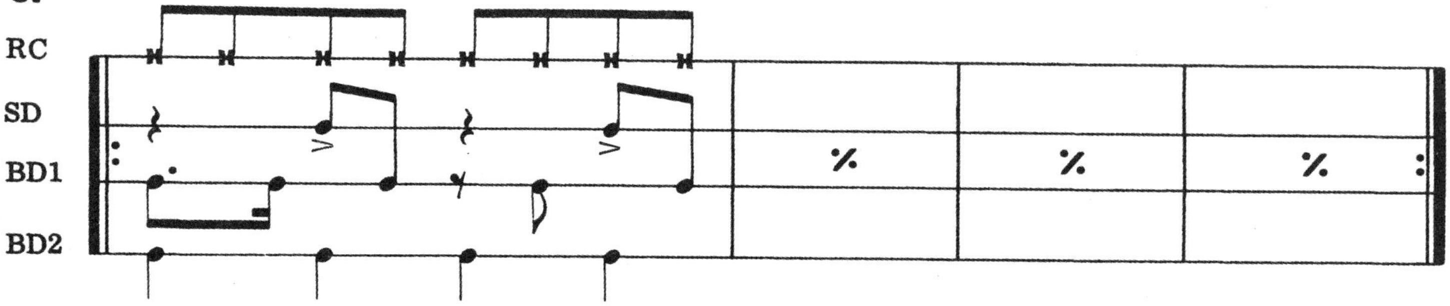

RC
SD
BD1
BD2

4.

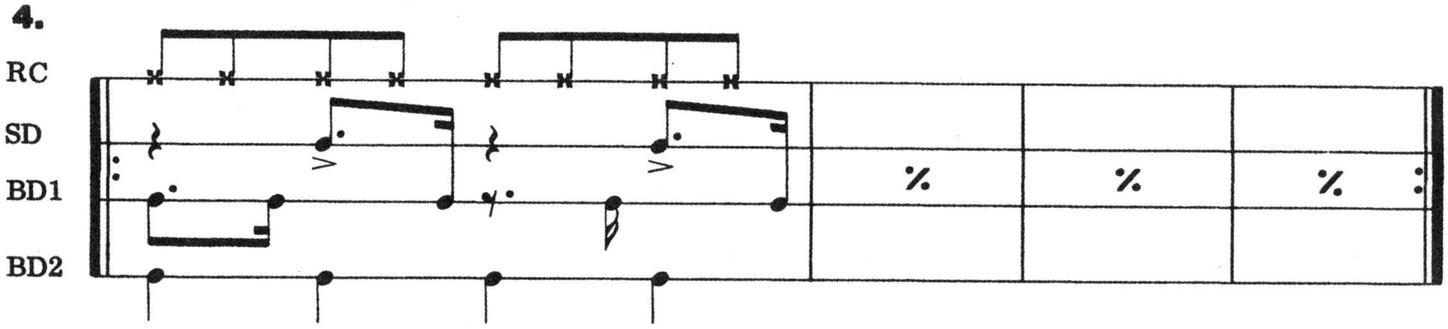

RC
SD
BD1
BD2

5.

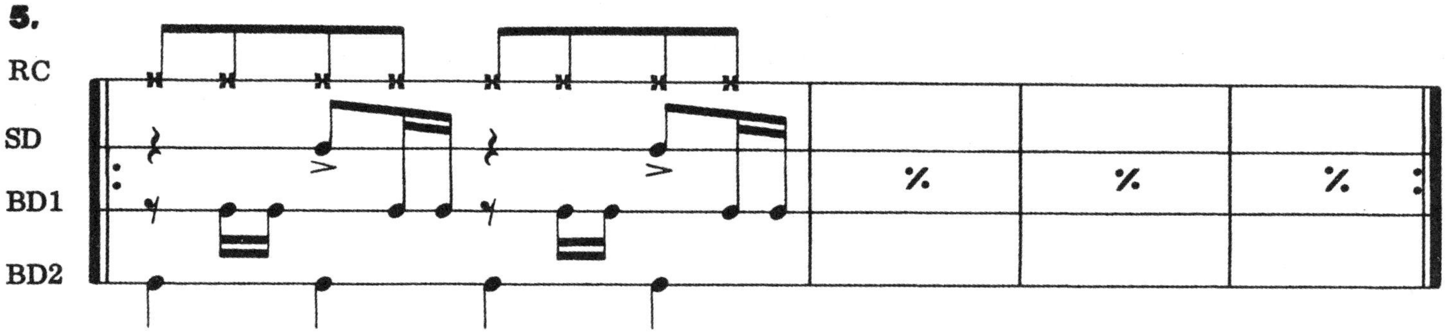

RC
SD
BD1
BD2

More Double Bass Rock Rhythms

(Using Quarter Notes on BD2)

6.

RC
SD
BD1
BD2

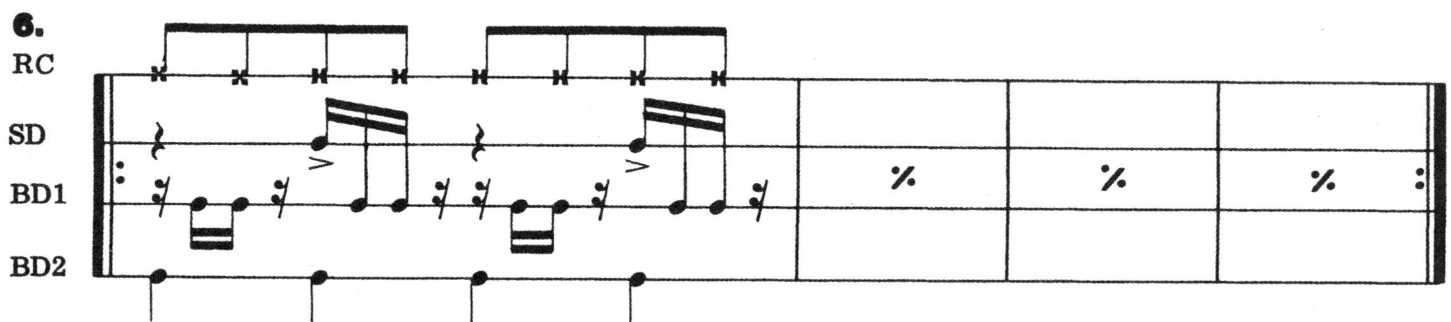

7.

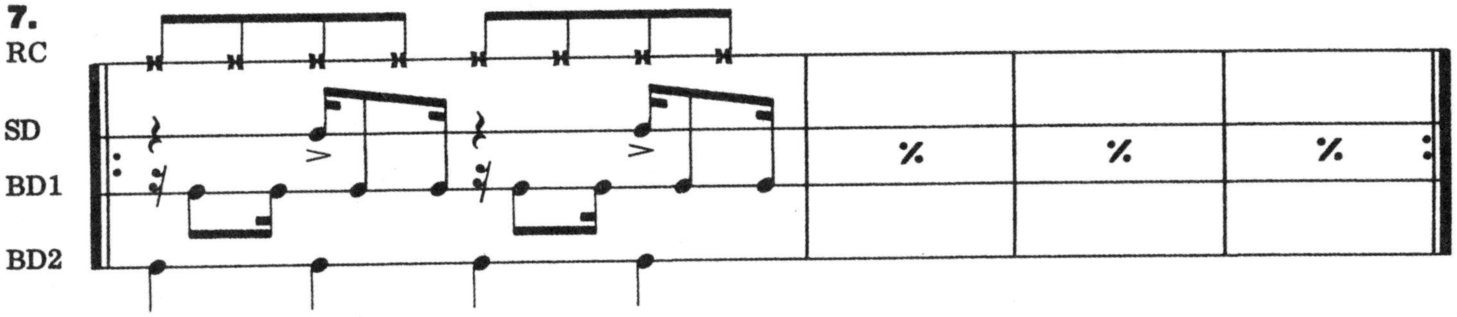

RC
SD
BD1
BD2

8.

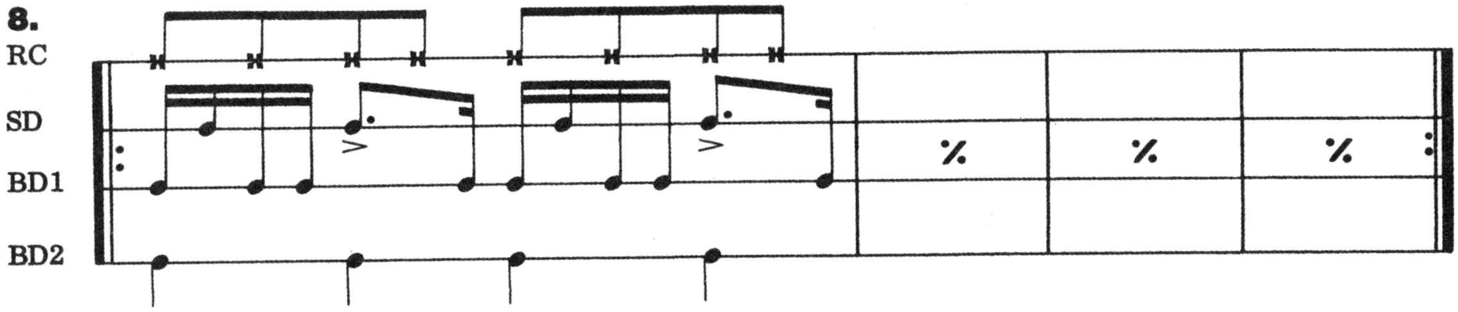

RC
SD
BD1
BD2

9.

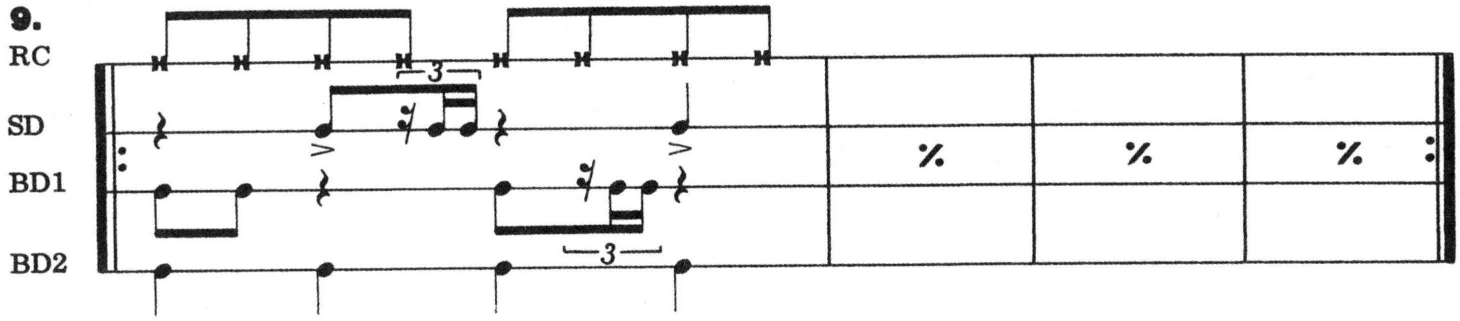

RC
SD
BD1
BD2

10.

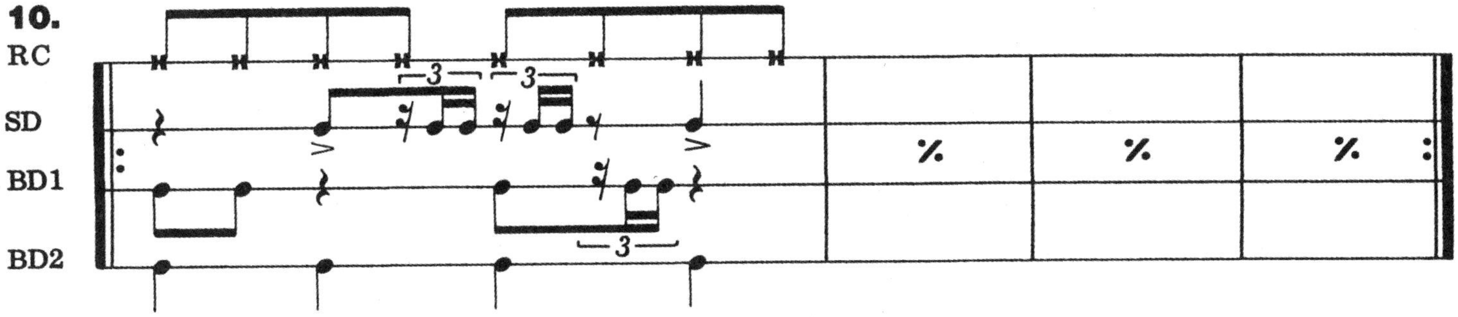

RC
SD
BD1
BD2

BD2 and BD1 Together as a Unit

Snare Drum on Each Beat

1.

RC
SD
BD1
BD2

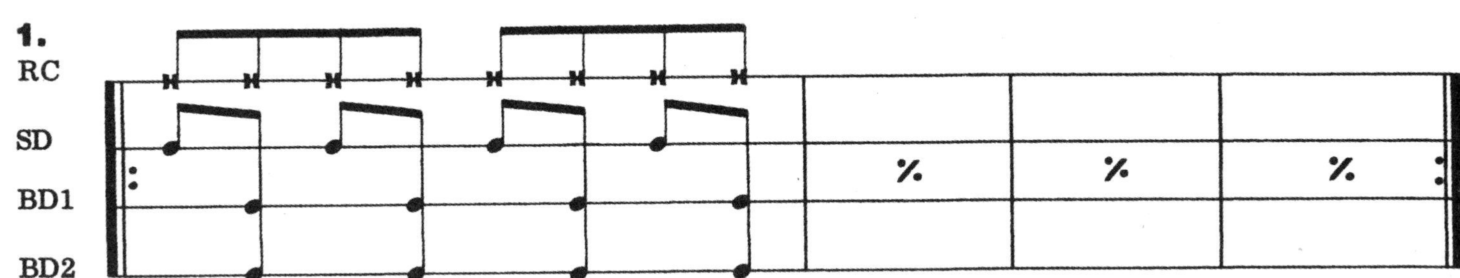

* For extra heavy rhythms of the feet.

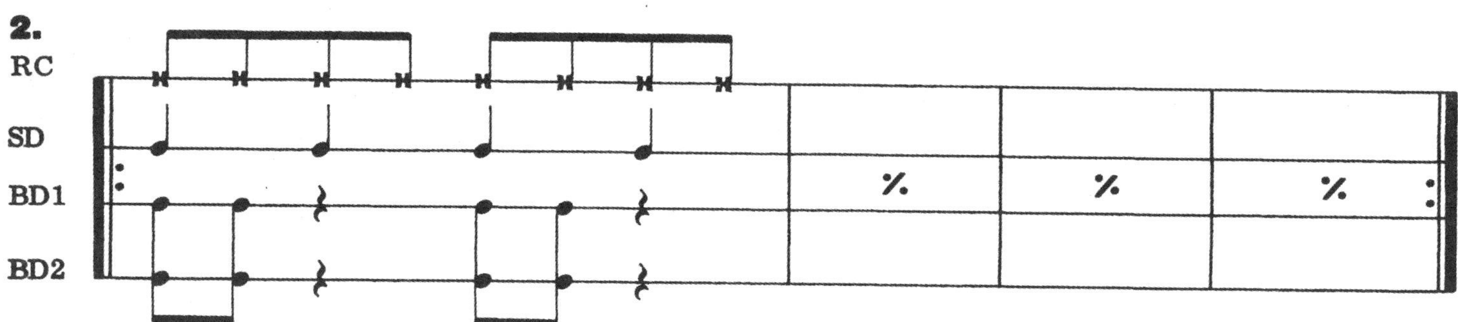
2.
RC
SD
BD1
BD2

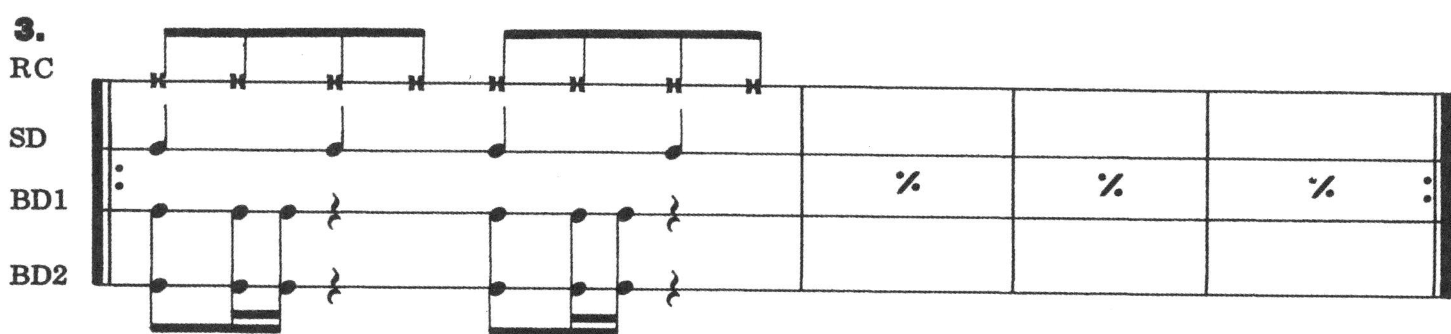
3.
RC
SD
BD1
BD2

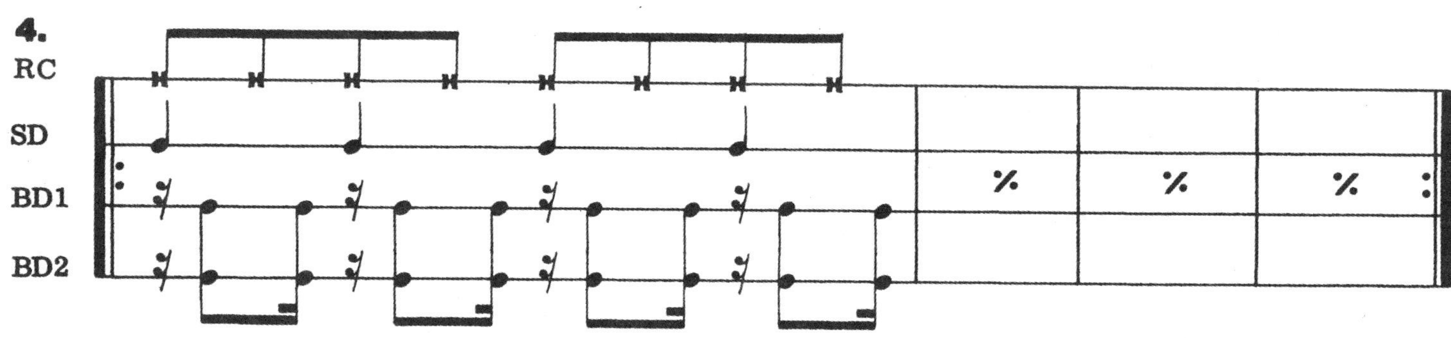
4.
RC
SD
BD1
BD2

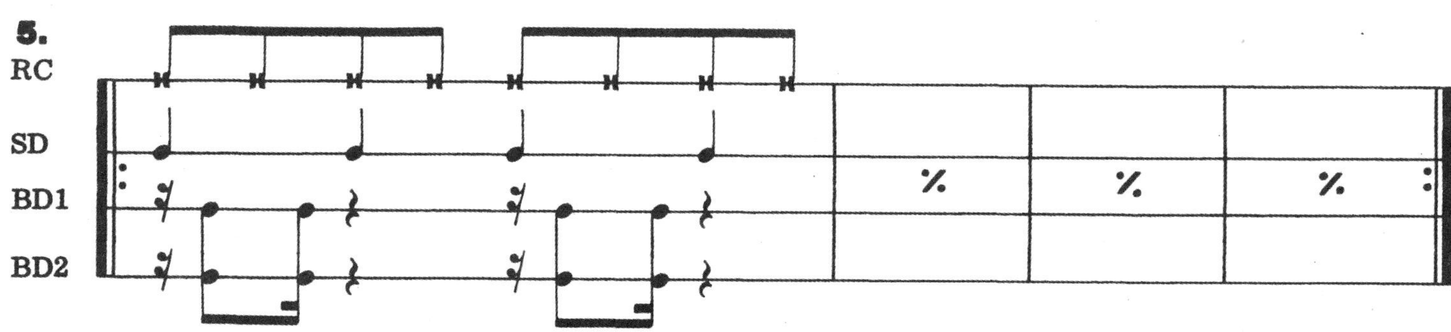
5.
RC
SD
BD1
BD2

BD2 and BD1 — Together

Snare Drum on 2 and 4

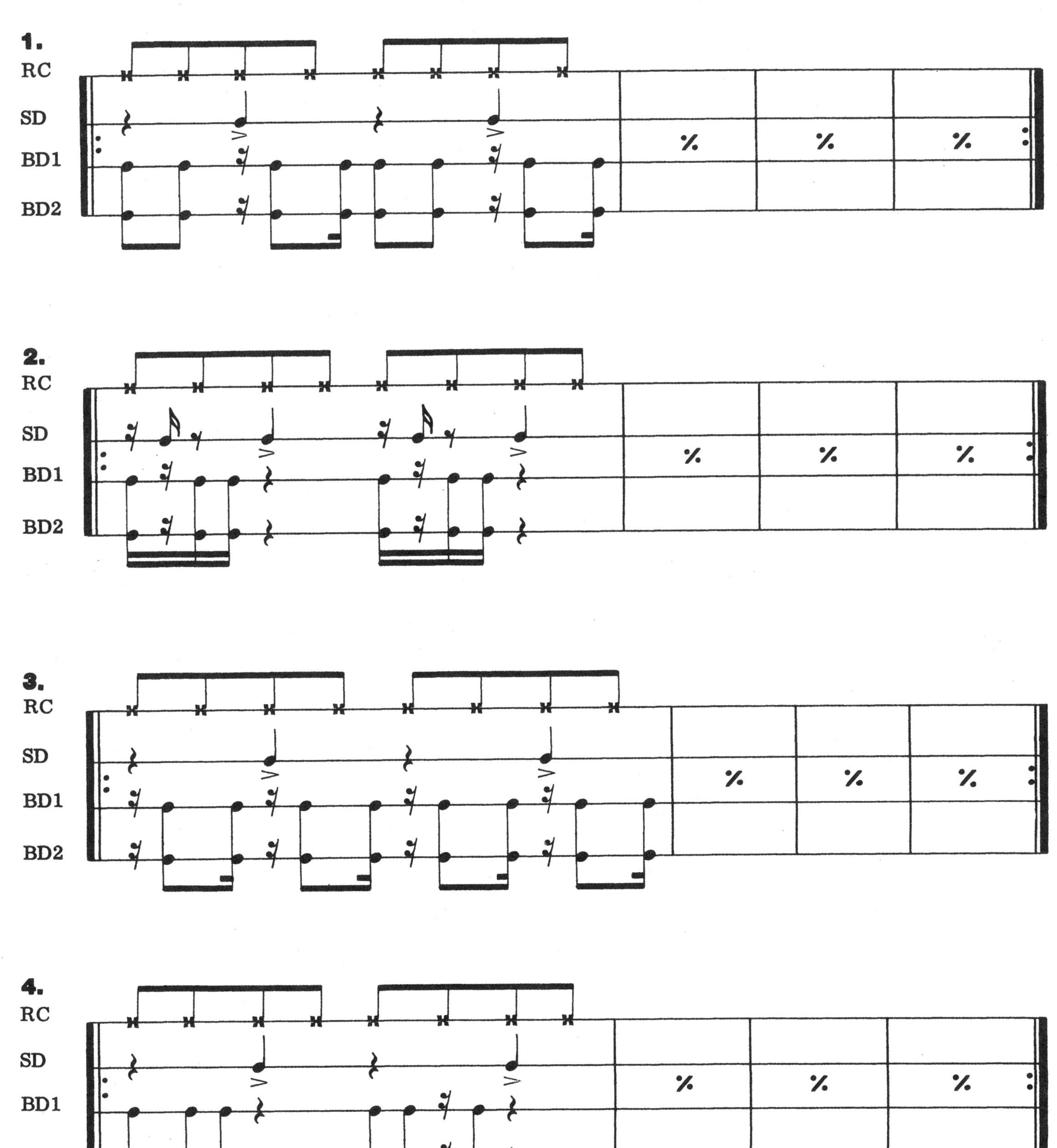

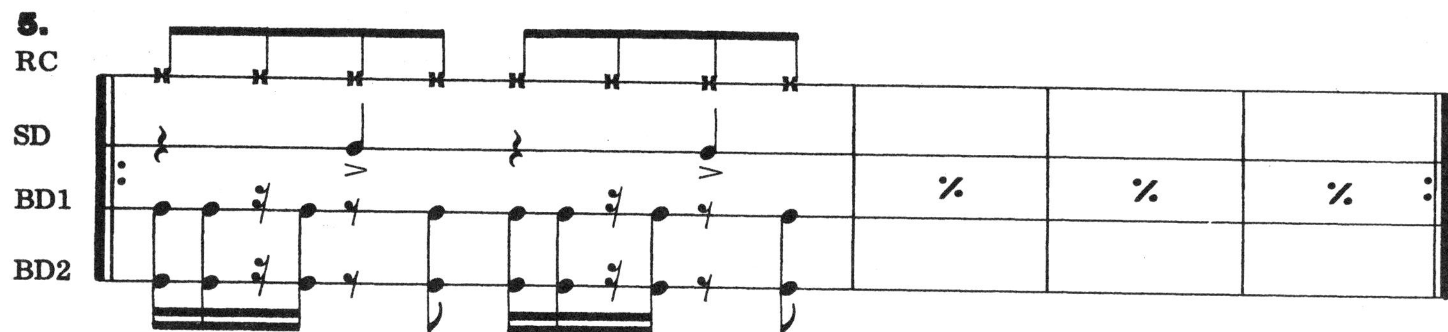

Sixteen Bar Exercise

RC
SD
BD1
BD2

3
3
3
3
3

Audio

Part 13

Realistic Linear Rudiments

The definition of linear is...Nothing hits together. Until now we've played patterns where different limbs play at the same time as other limbs. The following exercises will give you a new outlook on playing and will open up many new concepts for you to play.

Linear Rudiments

These rudiments should be practiced slowly at first, and gradually speed them up. These are LINEAR GROUPINGS as well as rudiments. A grouping is a group of notes that when played create a phrase or melody.

R = RIGHT HAND L = LEFT HAND Ⓕ = FOOT

A- The Three note grouping = R L Ⓕ
1 2 3

B- Four note grouping R L L Ⓕ
1 2 3 4

Use a metronome playing quarter notes to practice to!!!!

C- The Five = R L R R Ⓕ Play hand to hand over and over.
L R L L Ⓕ
1 2 3 4 5

D- The Six = R L R L L Ⓕ repeat over and over
1 2 3 4 5 6

Now, practice these very seriously because these patterns are the basis for linear playing.

Putting It Together

Let's put some of these rudiments together so we can use them as grooves and fills. The first combination we will use is using the 7 and 9 grouping.

The six and three together = the nine grouping. 9= R L R L L Ⓕ R L Ⓕ repeat, etc.
1 2 3 4 5 6 7 8 9

The four and three together = the seven grouping. 7= R L L Ⓕ R L Ⓕ repeat etc.

All linear rudiments can be played as follows to create independence. P:actice all of the following ways:

1-Rights Bass Drum (right foot when you see the " Ⓕ ").

2-Left Bass Drum (left foot when you see the " Ⓕ ").

3-Alternate Bass Drums (if your first hit is a right the next Bass Drum (BD) hit is a left etc.) You can also use your left foot on your Hi-Hat.

How To Use These Rudiments

Now, in 4/4 time there are 16 sixteenth notes to a bar. So let's count our LINEAR GROUPINGS as 16th notes. We need two groupings that would sub-divide into 16. A good one to start with is the 7 and 9, together they equal 16, which equals one bar. The syncopation created by this combination is what makes this stuff interesting, fresh and new. Below are some examples of this concept: play them slow at first, then build up speed.

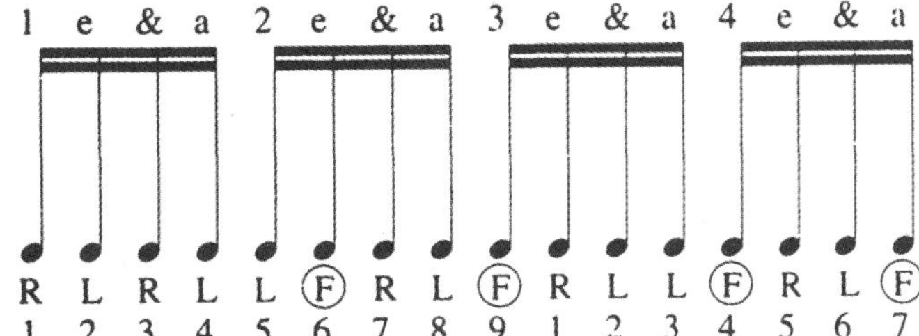

9+7=16 notes Repeat etc.

Two bar phrases sound great doing these patterns. Here are some two bar combinations. Thirty-two sixteenth notes.

2- Repeat #1 for two bars = 9-7 9-7 and play over and over. Put two bars of straight time in between the LINEAR GROUPING patterns.

2a- You can do 9-7 or reverse it to 7-9; it still has the same total of notes. (1 bar =16, 2 bars =32).

Here is the 9-7 (A), and 7-9 (B) sequences. Play A & B together as a two bar phrase

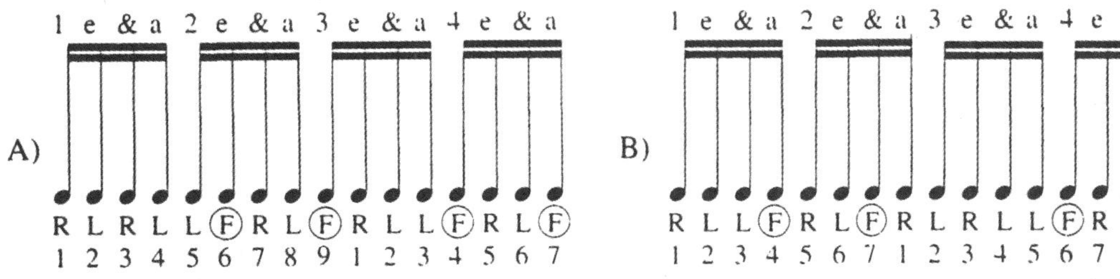

1-Once you get these down, put your right hand on the Hi-Hat, the left hand on the snare drum and play the exercise.

2-Put your left hand on the Hi-Hat and your right hand on the snare and Toms. This will create a different variation of syncopation.

Here are some more LINEAR GROUPING combinations to try: (2 bars).

#5) 9-9/7-7 #6) 7-7/9-9 #7) 7-7-2/9-7 #8) 5-5-1 (one bar)

#9) 4 bars 64 -16th notes: 4 bars 7-7-7-7 7-7-7-7-7-1 = 4 Bars
9 x 7 + 1 = 64 sixteenth notes

NOTE: Use a metronome playing quarter notes to practice.

There are two play-along tracks included here, with no drums. Choose some of your favorite beats and play along to "Everybody's Comin'" and "Gray Day," which are in 4/4!

This page has been left open for you to write your own rhythms. Good luck, and have fun!

Audio - Everybody's Comin'

Audio - Gray Day

RC
SD
BD

RC
SD
BD

RC
SD
BD

RC
SD
BD

RC
SD
BD

RC
SD
BD

Part 14

Realistic Rock 7/8 Timing

Welcome to the odd time signatures of Realistic Rock. In this section we will learn how to play in 7/8 and 9/8 time signatures. These two odd time signatures are very close when learning to play them. What makes them different are two eighth notes.

Our first odd time signature will be 7/8.

In 4/4 we have eight eighth notes in one bar and in 7/8 we have seven eighth notes in one bar.

Counting out loud and repeating each count will only increase your ability to feel natural with these odd time signatures. Once comfortable, each downbeat will be easily anticipated as if you were playing in 4/4. Emphasizing the one of each count with your bass drum will speed up the process!

The count is simple: **1, 2, 3, 4, 5, 6, sev,**... saying **SEV** instead of seven makes it easier to count so that all the counts are one syllable.

Remember—count over and over… **1, 2, 3, 4, 5, 6, sev, 1, 2, 3, 4, 5, 6, sev,** etc.

It is important to note that the 7/8 grooves will change the note values in relation to 4/4.

Example:

Eighth notes = one beat
Sixteenth notes = half a beat
Eighth notes are now counted **1, 2, 3, 4, 5, 6, sev.**
Sixteenth notes are now counted **1 &, 2 &, 3 &, 4 &, 5 &, 6 &, 7 &,** etc.
Sixteenth note triplets are now counted **1 & a, 2 & a, 3 & a, 4 & a, 5 & a, 6 & a, 7 & a,** etc.

In order to make each exercise easier to read, think of them as bars of 4/4 stopping on the count of four and where the & of four should be we now think of it as beat one... in other words, we cut off the last eighth note of the 4/4 bar.

Count **1 &, 2 &, 3 &, 4, 1 &, 2 &, 3 &, 4**—no space between **4** and **1**... when counting, as previously mentioned, emphasize the count of one (downbeat) with your bass drum in order to feel comfortable with the 7/8 time signature.

Good luck... now go to **Ex.1** and have some fun!

Realistic 7/8 Time—Eighth Notes

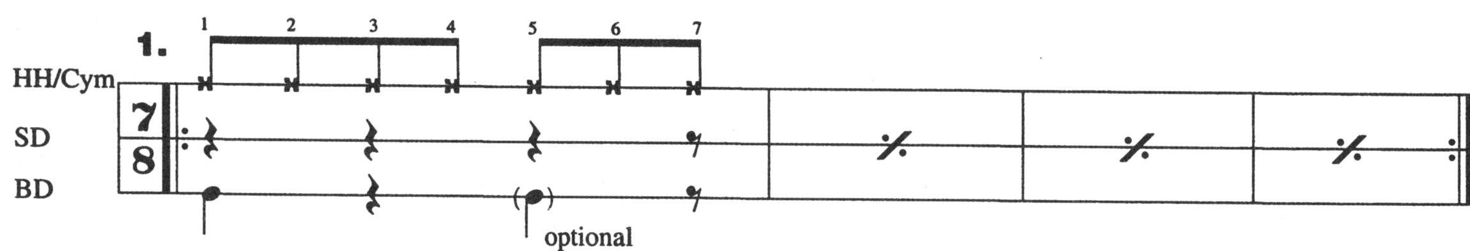

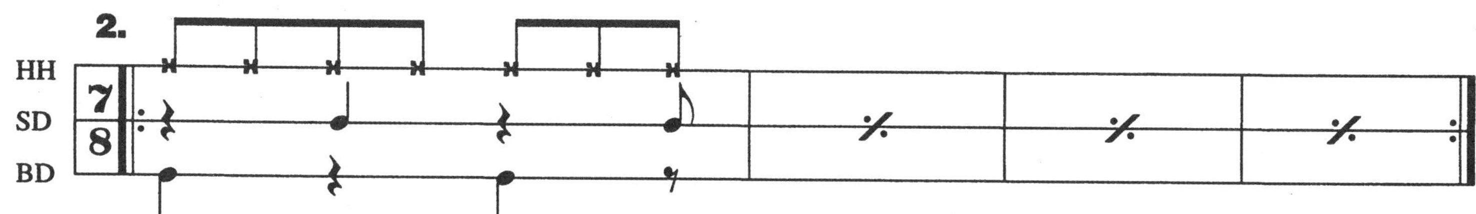

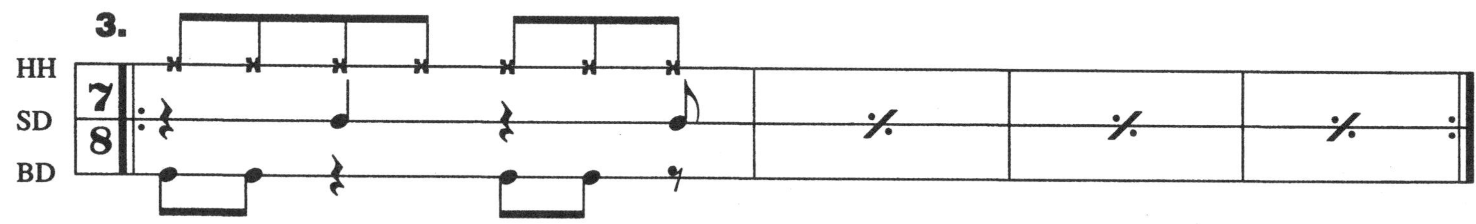

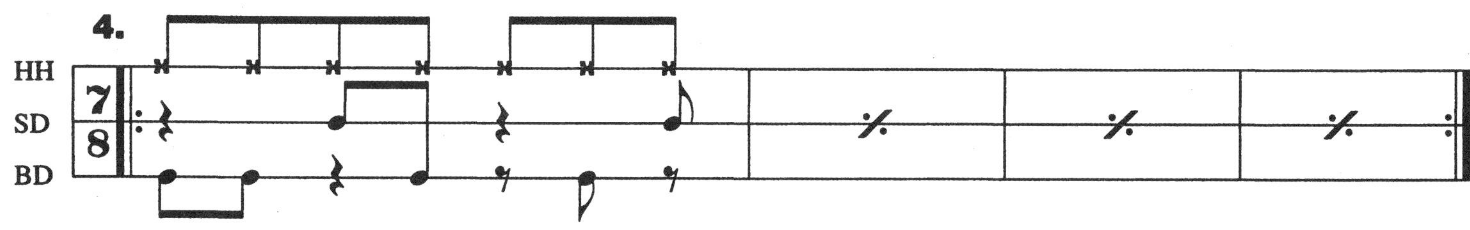

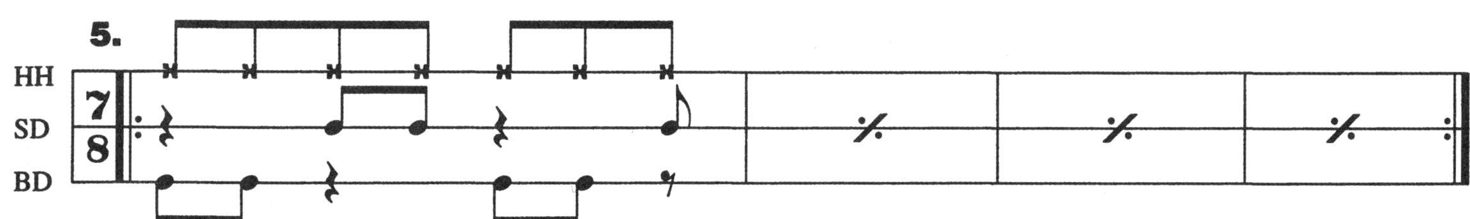

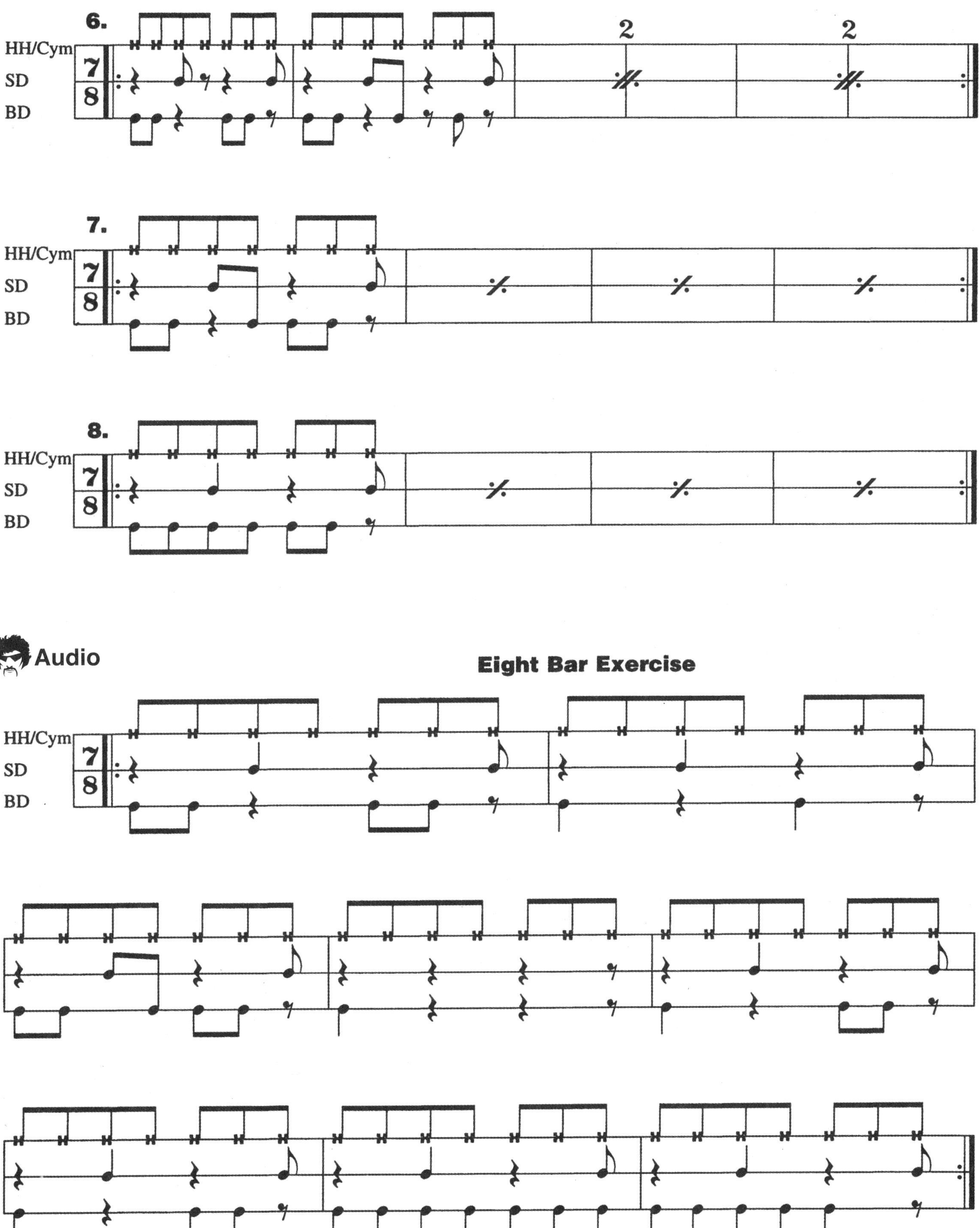
6.
HH/Cym
SD
BD
7
8
2
2
7.
HH/Cym
SD
BD
7
8
8.
HH/Cym
SD
BD
7
8
Audio
Eight Bar Exercise
HH/Cym
SD
BD
7
8

Realistic 7/8 Time—Sixteenth Notes

1.
HH/Cym
SD
BD

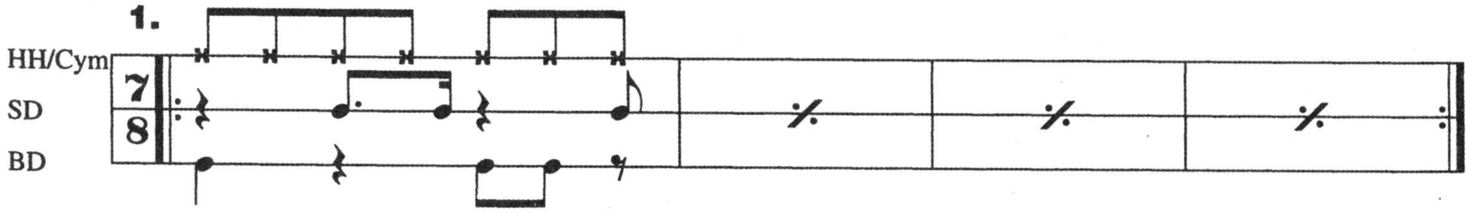

2.
HH
SD
BD

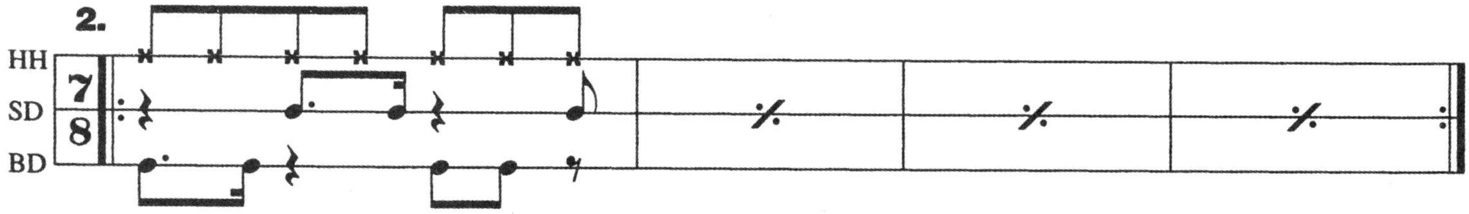

3.
HH
SD
BD

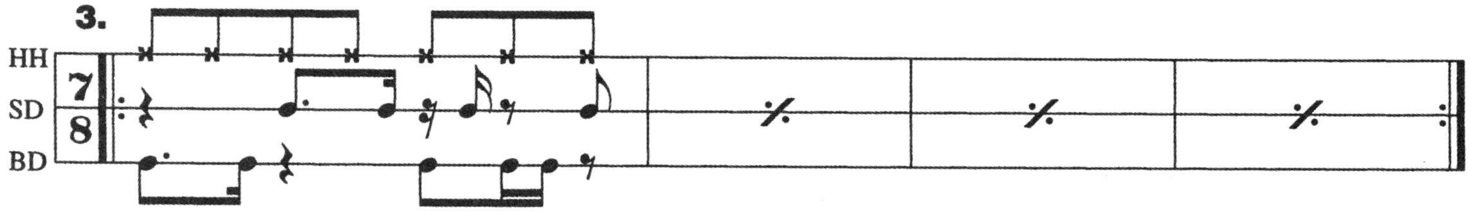

4.
HH
SD
BD

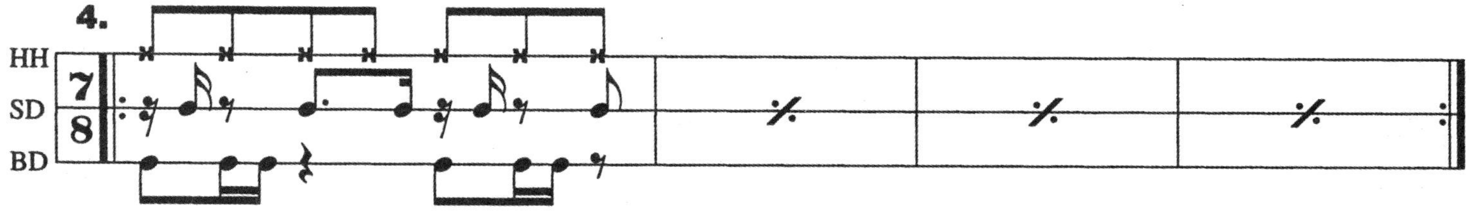

5.
HH
SD
BD

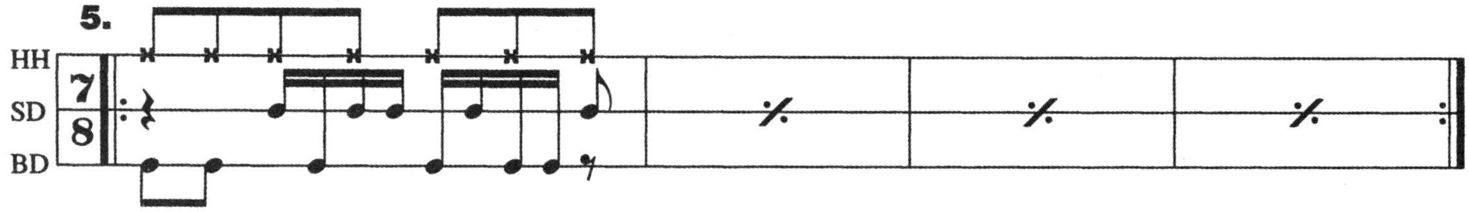

6.
HH
SD
BD

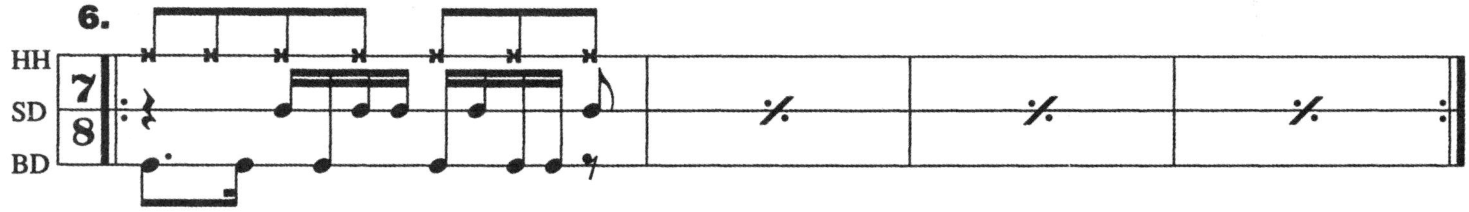

7.
HH
SD
BD

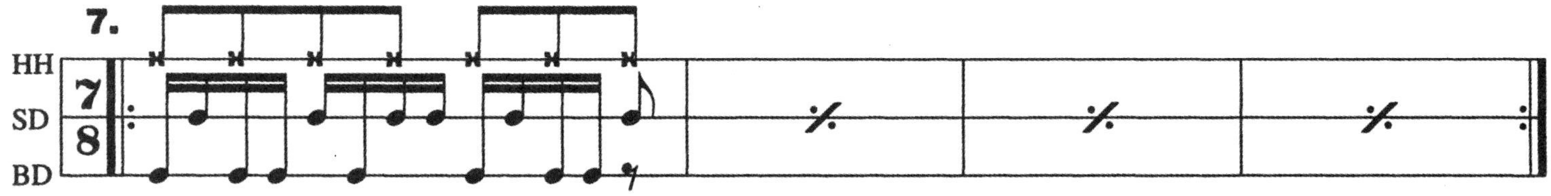

7/8 Time—Sixteenth Notes

7/8 Bonus Groove
7/8 Against 4 on the Snare

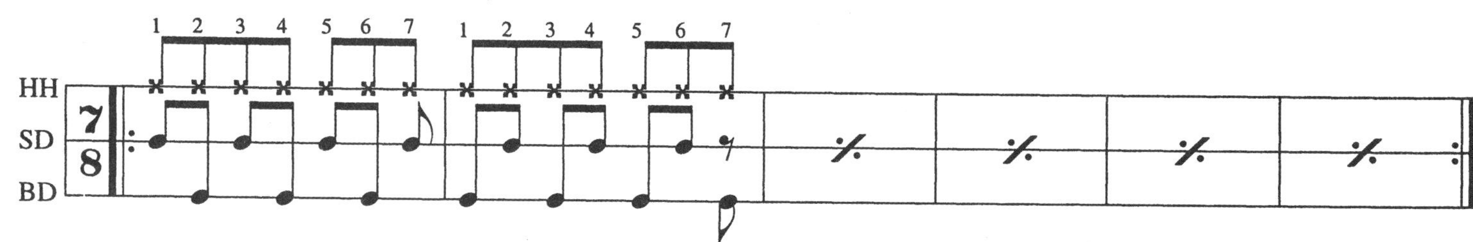

The above exercise creates a 4/4 feel on the snare even though we are playing in 7/8. This technique can and should be applied to all odd time signatures... 7/8 - 9/8 - 11/8 - 13/8, etc.

Audio

7/8 Fills

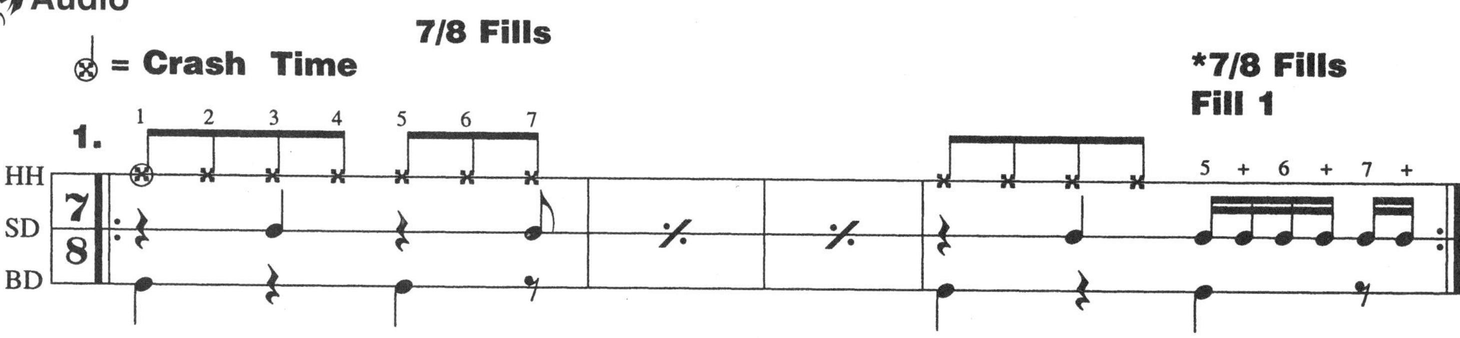

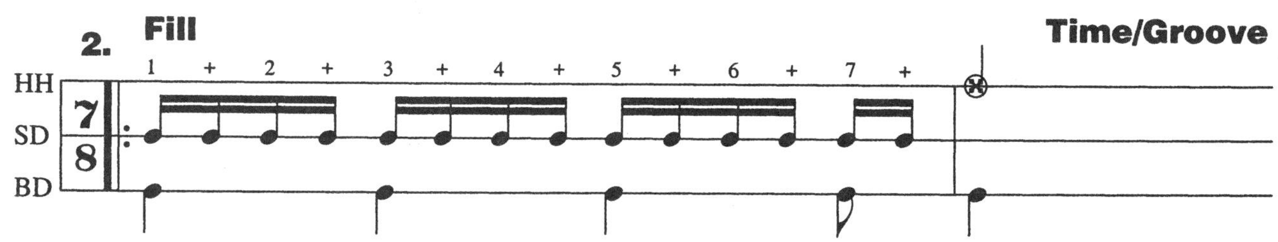

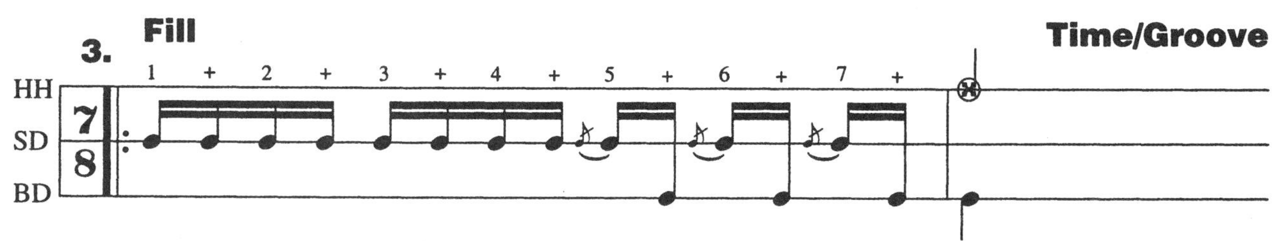

* Play fill and then play time.

7/8 Drum Fills

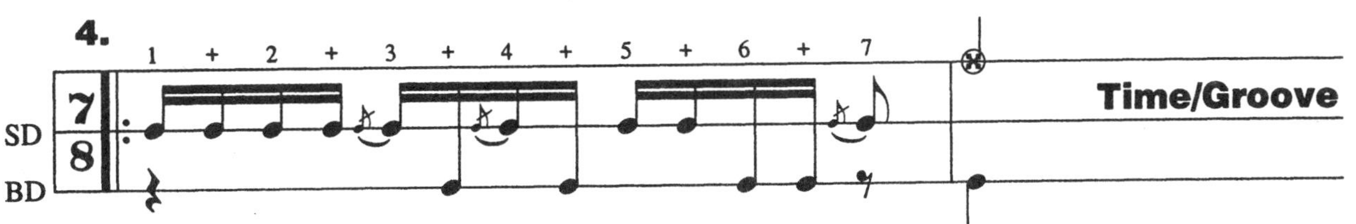

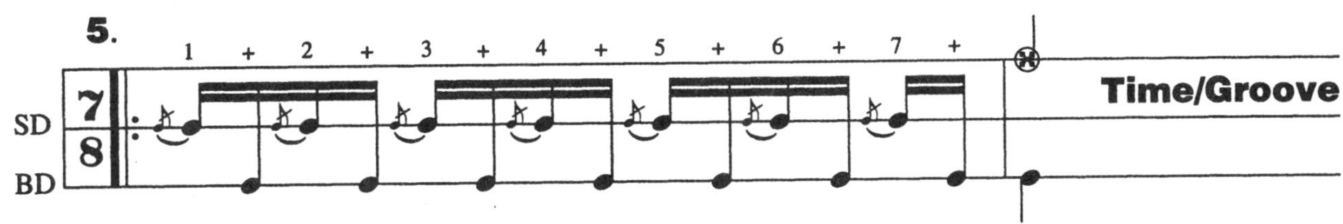

Audio

7/8 to 4/4—Four Bar Phrases

1.

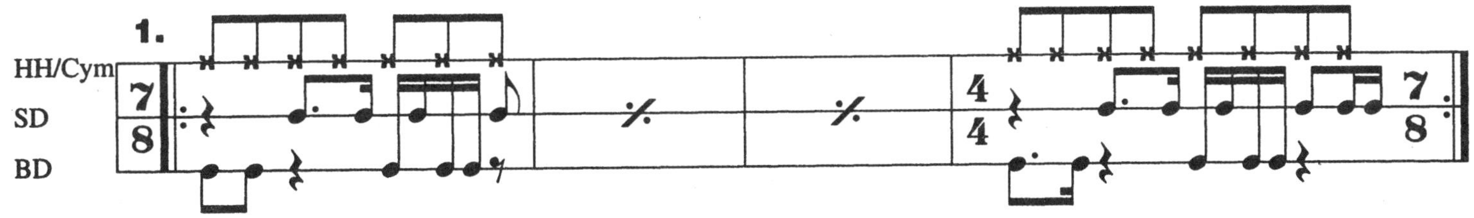

HH/Cym
SD
BD

2.

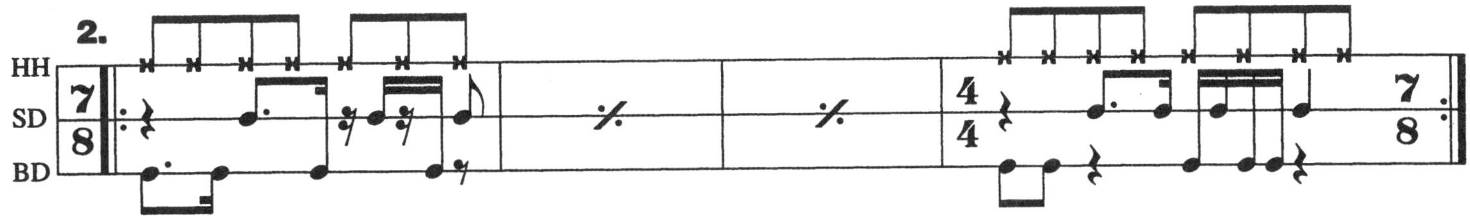

HH
SD
BD

3.

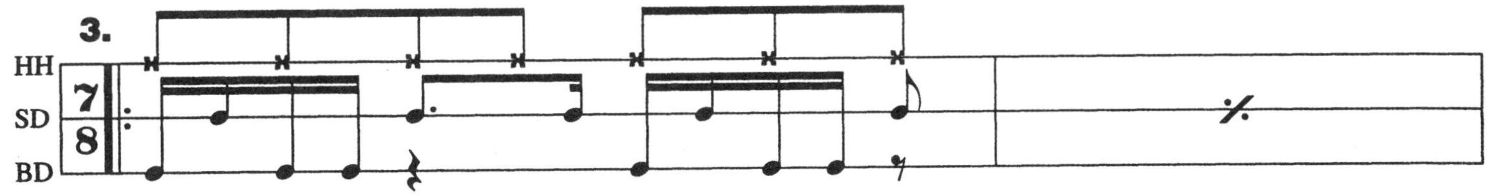

HH
SD
BD

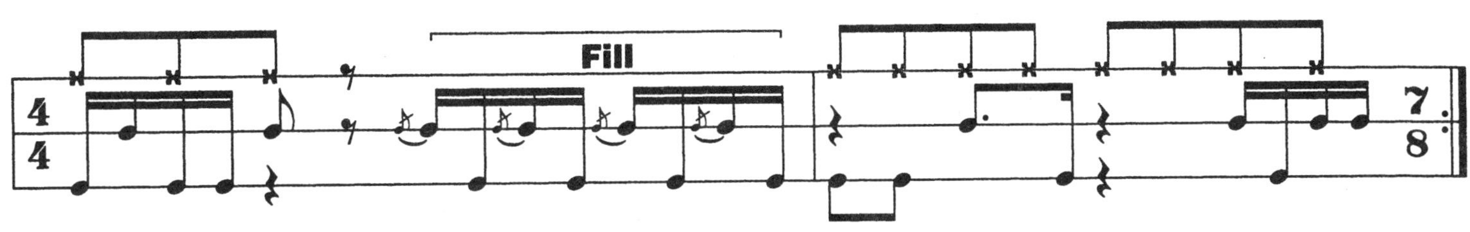

7/8 Drum Solo

7/8 Bonus Groove

Note: On **CD 1** there is a **Play-along song** called **STASH.**
The solo is played as three bars of **7/8** and one bar of **4/4.**
Here is an example of the three bars of **7/8** and one bar of **4/4** on the **CD 1** play-along **STASH.**

Part 15

Realistic Rock 9/8 Timing

Now that you have finished the 7/8 exercises it is time to add the two eighth notes we talked about and have some fun with 9/8!

In 9/8, just like 7/8, the eighth notes are counted as one beat. There are nine eighth notes to a bar. The count is **1, 2, 3, 4, 5, 6, sev(7), 8, 9.**

Once again, keep counting out loud so that the time becomes automatic and you can feel each downbeat naturally!

Count this over and over... **1, 2, 3, 4, 5, 6, sev(7), 8, 9, 1, 2, 3, 4, 5, 6, sev(7), 8, 9,** etc.

With each count, remember to play your bass drum on the count of one (downbeat) in order to feel comfortable with 9/8, just like the way we practiced in the 7/8 section.

Once again, the eighth note gets a full beat and the sixteenth note gets half a beat. You should have the idea by now, if not, go back to the 7/8 text and review.

9/8 is the same as playing one bar of 4/4 except you now add one eighth note and count **1 &, 2 &, 3 &, 4 &, 5**—the count stops on the fifth beat... there is no **&** of **5**—the count starts over again after **5** and then immediately back to **1.**

Go for it... **Good Luck!**

Realistic 9/8 Time—Eighth Notes

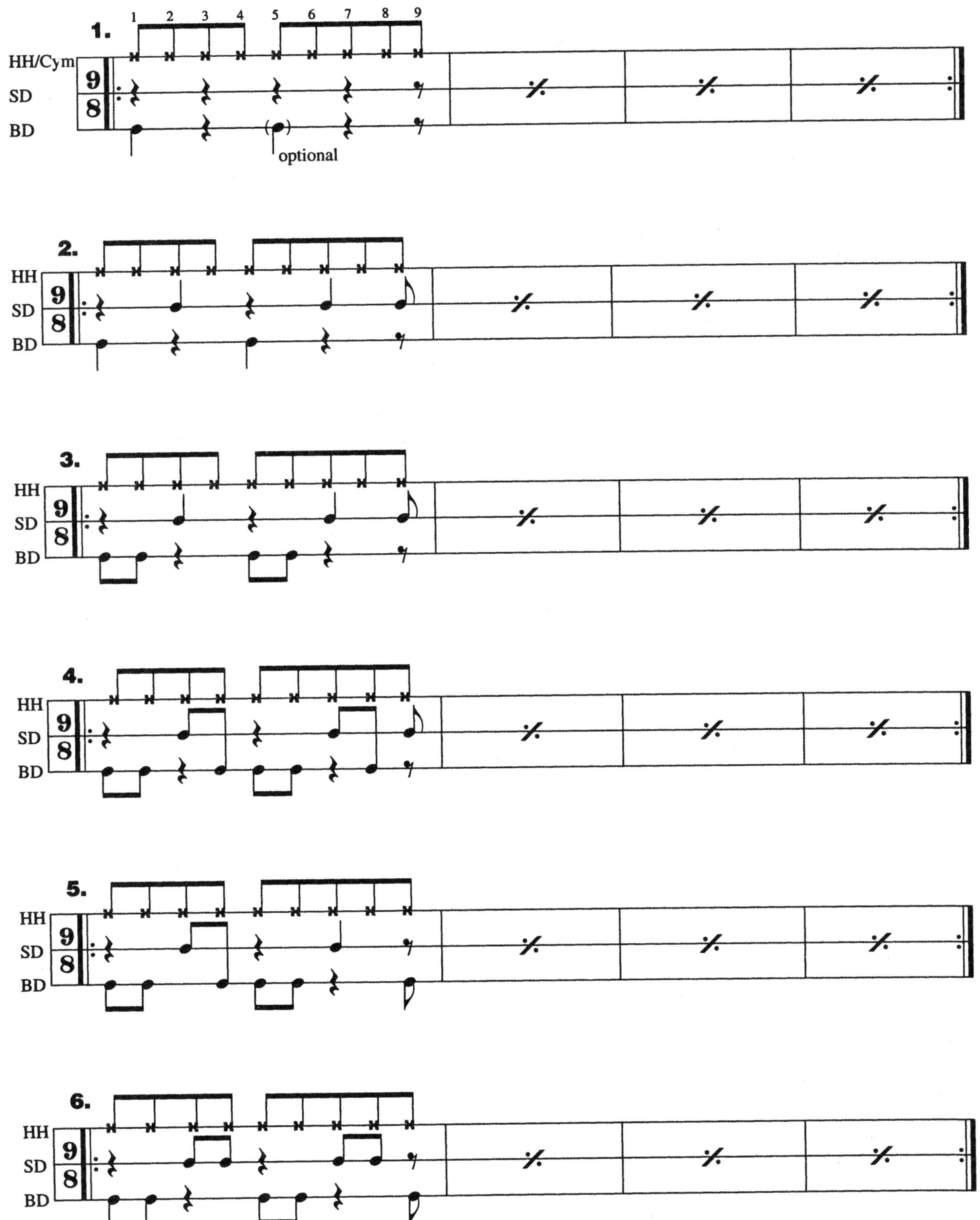

7.

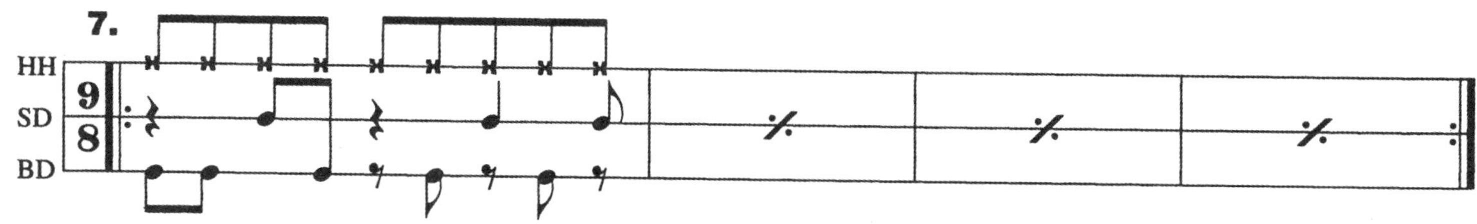

8.

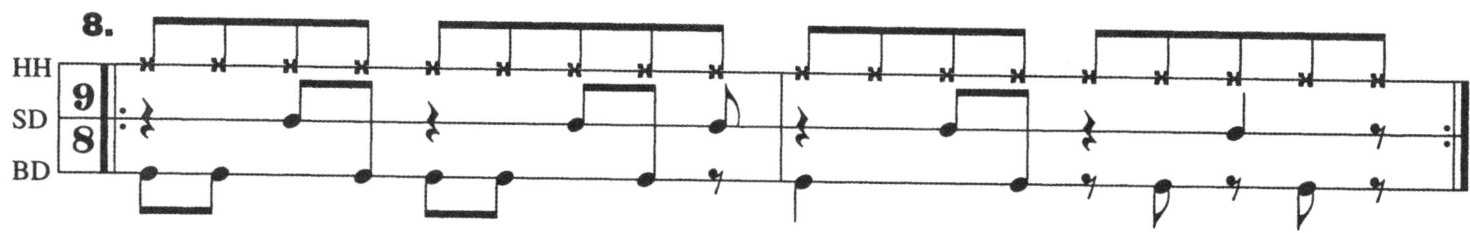

Audio

Eight Bar Exercise

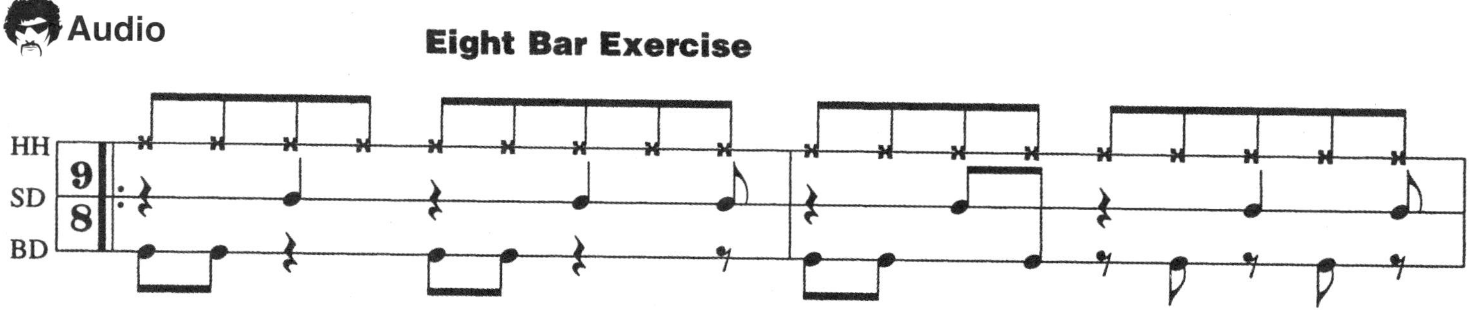

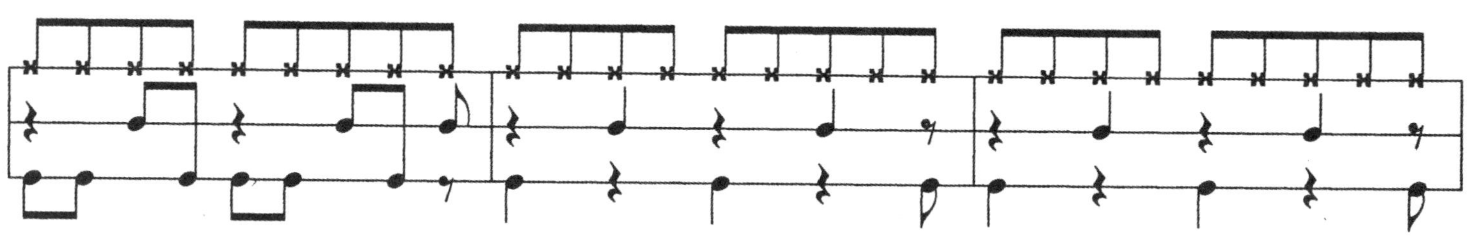

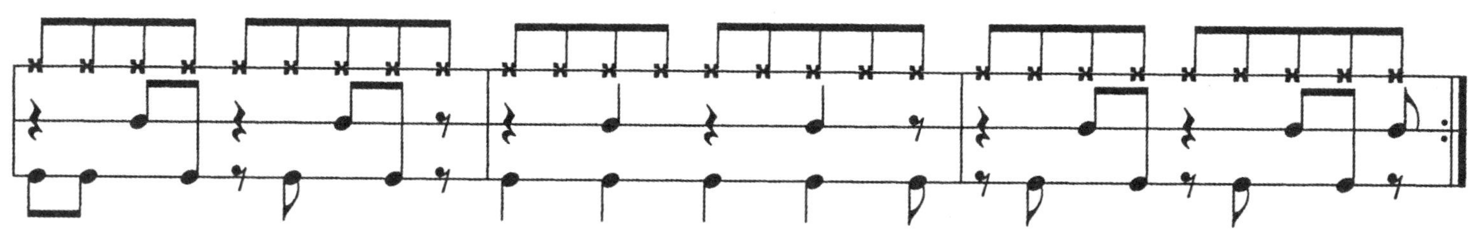

Note: Bars seven and eight imply a 4/4 time signature in the bass drum while playing in 9/8.

Realistic 9/8 Time—Sixteenth Notes

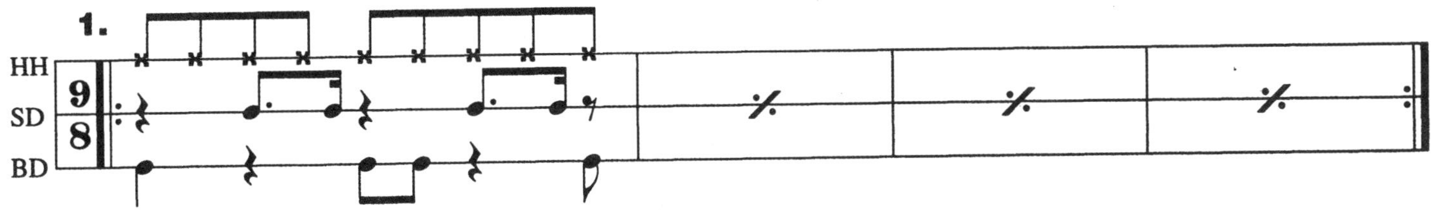

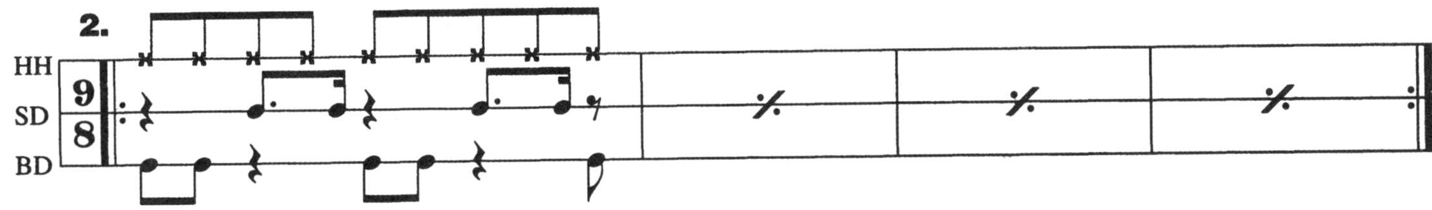

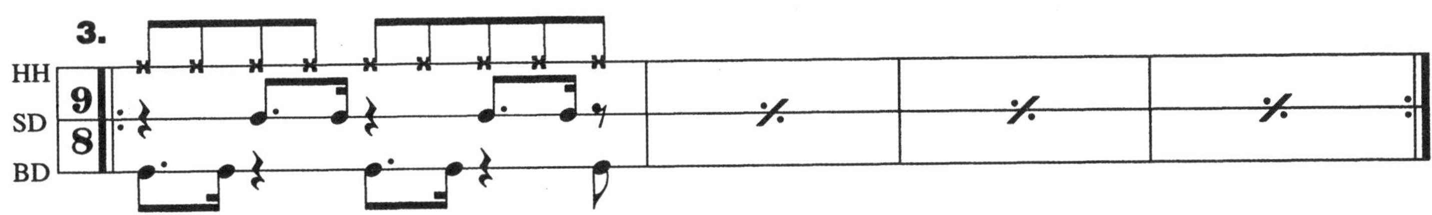

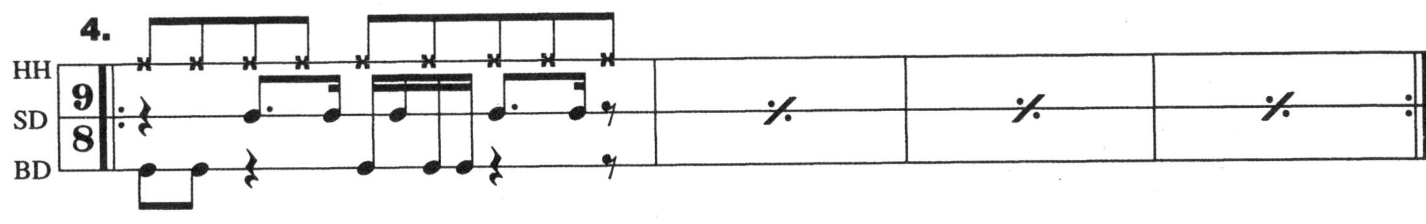

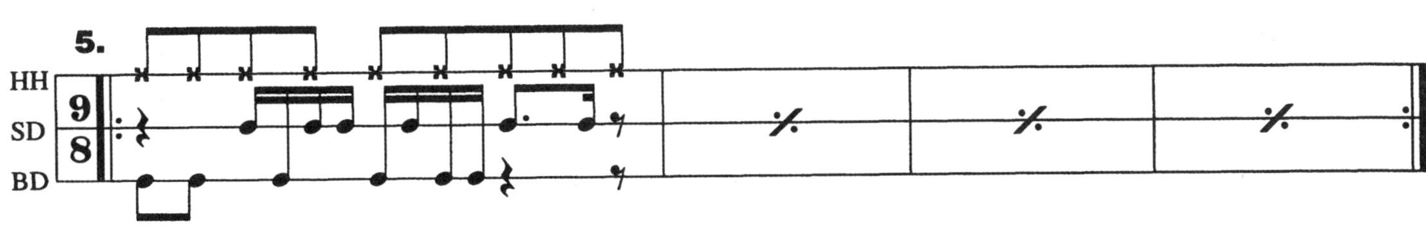

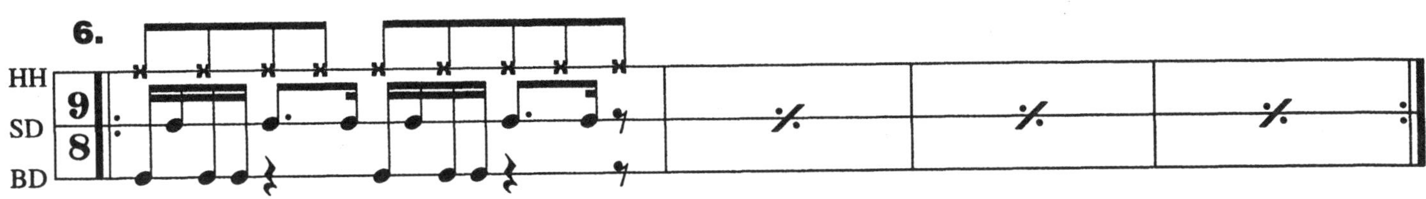

7.
HH
SD
BD
8.
HH
SD
BD
9.
HH
SD
BD
10.
HH
SD
BD
Audio
Eight Bar Exercise
HH
SD
BD

9/8 Against 4 on the Snare
9/8 Bonus

Audio

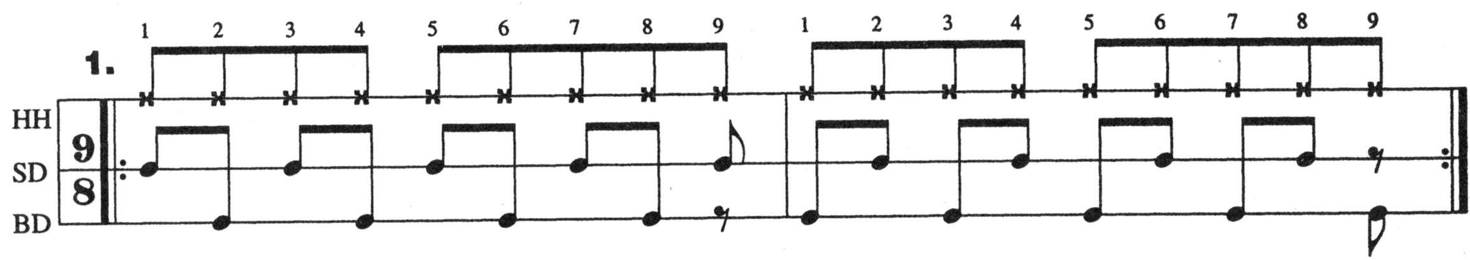

Note: The snare plays on all of the downbeats in the first bar and then automatically switches to the off-beats in the second bar.

Audio

9/8 Drum Fills

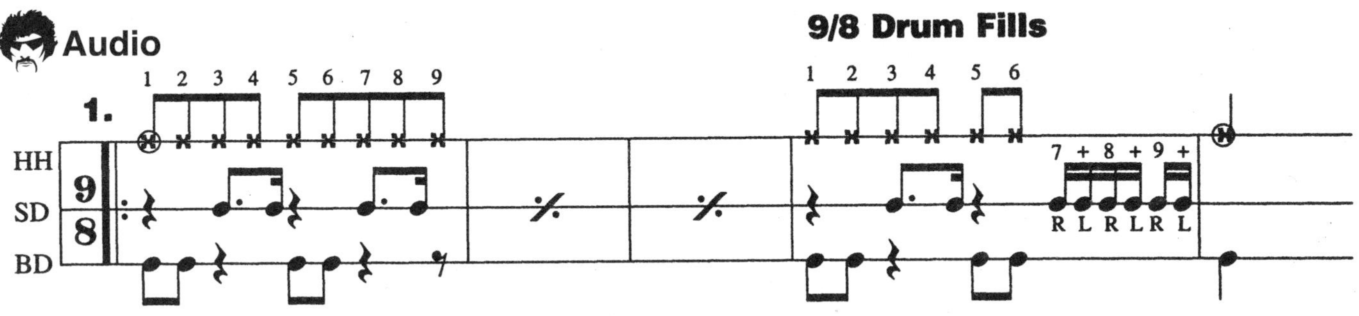

***Fills**

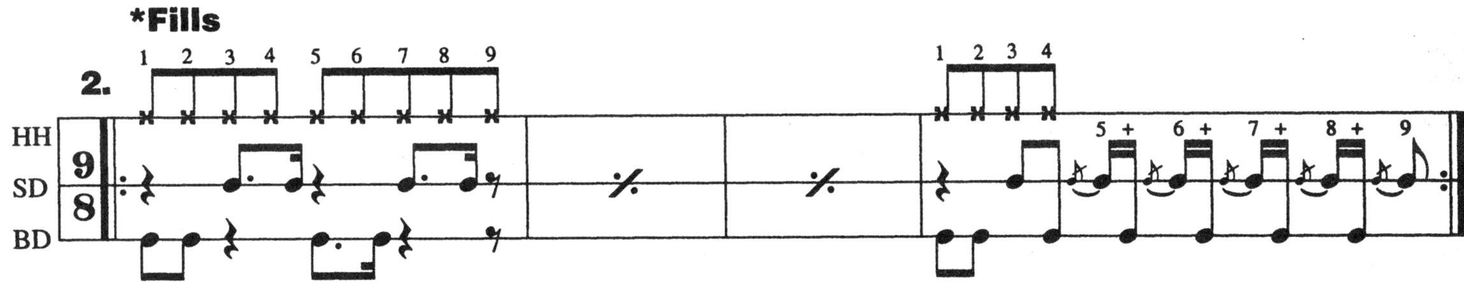

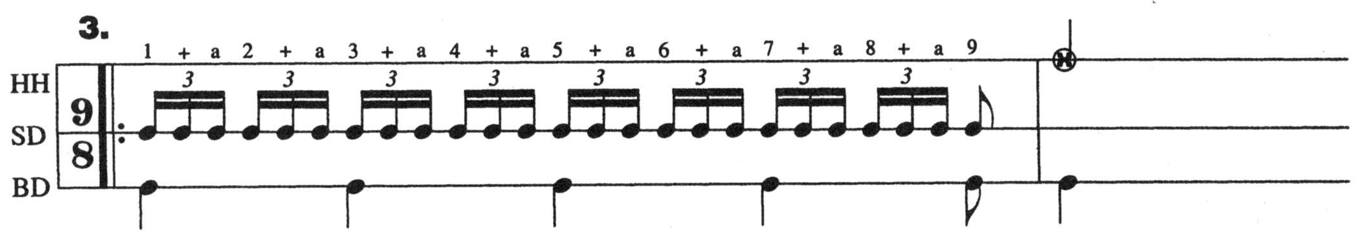

* Play Groove and apply fills then back to Groove.

Realistic Rock 9/8
9/8 to 4/4 Time

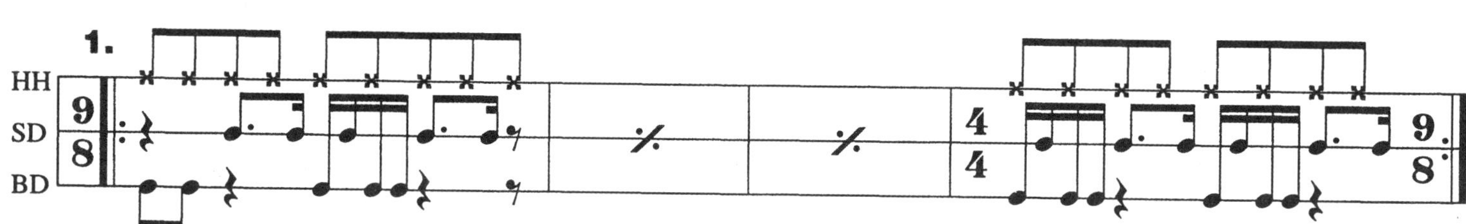

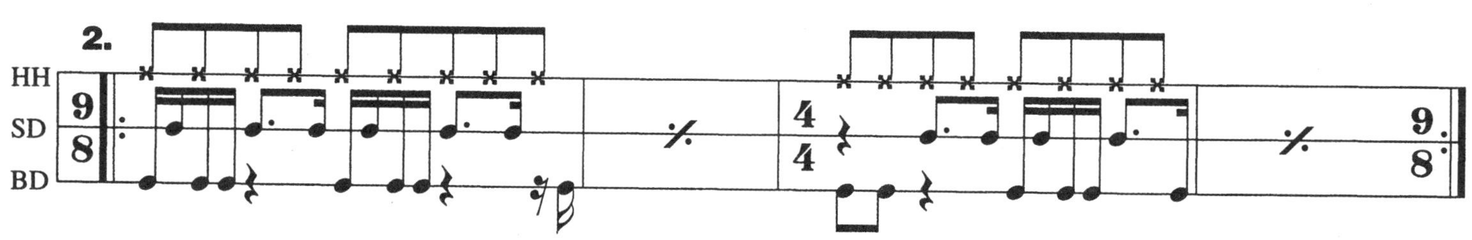

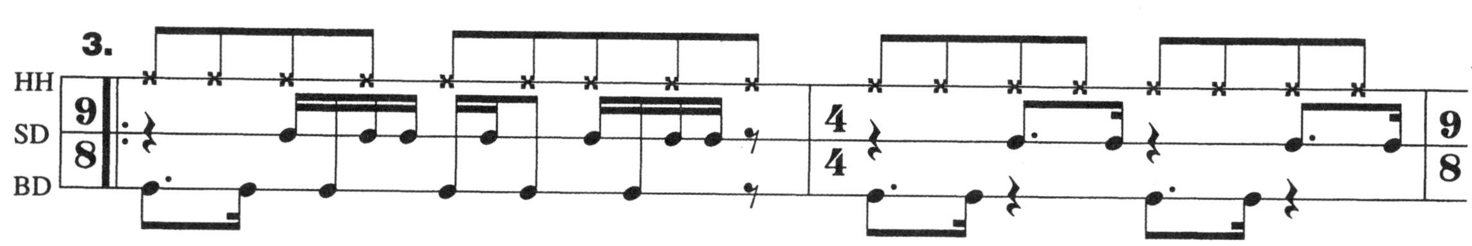

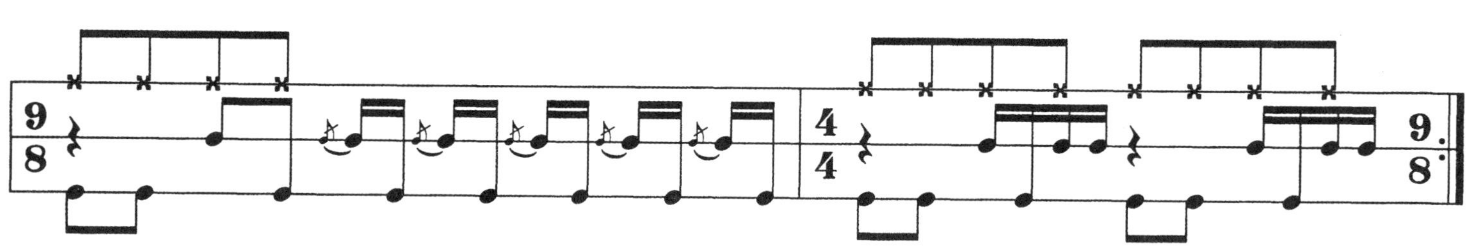

Audio

9/8 Drum Solo

Part 16

Combinations

Audio

Cymbals/Snare Drum

In this section we will explore various hand and foot combinations that can be played in a variety of musical situations.

Here we will present these "cutting edge" combinations as drum fills using triplets and sixteenth notes. Once you are comfortable with them, you will quickly discover how melodic and powerful your drumming will become which is a trademark of all great rock drummers!

Combination #1

Each exercise will include the count with the appropriate sticking and foot combination written underneath. Play them as sixteenth notes with an **even** and **steady** flow!

Ex. 1

	1	**e**	**&**	**a**	**2**	**e**	**&**	**a**	**3**	**e**	**repeat over and over**
	1	2	1	2	1	2	1	2	3	4	
Hands	R	L			R	L					
Feet			R	L			R	L	R	L	

Audio

Practice slowly at first then build up speed.

Ex. 2 **Played as sixteenth notes**

	1	**e**	**&**	**a**	**2**	**e**	**&**	**a**	**3**	**e**	**&**	**a**	**4**	**e**	**&**	**a**	**repeat**
	1	2	1	2	1	2	1	2	3	4	1	2	1	2	3	4	
Hands	R	L			R	L					R	L					
Feet			R	L			R	L	R	L			R	L	R	L	

Audio

Practice slowly at first to build up speed.

Ex. 3

	1	**e**	**&**	**a**	**2**	**e**	**&**	**a**	**3**	**e**	**&**	**a**	**4**	**e**	**&**	**a**
	1	2	3	4	1	2	3	4	1	2	3	4	1	2	3	4
Hands	R	L	R	L					R	L	R	L				
Feet					R	L	R	L					R	L	R	L

Audio

Combinations #2

The combinations below are played with the hands on the snare or toms and two China cymbals. The China cymbals are to be played together with your bass drums. As you gradually increase your speed, the short "staccato" sound of the Chinas will help your momentum until you are playing these patterns as fast and as clean as you want.

In order to feel comfortable with these patterns, it is recommended that you first learn to play the patterns between the snare and the double bass drums and gradually introduce the China cymbals and then the toms.

These combinations are similar to Ex.1 except the bass drums are now answering the hand patterns.

Practice Between Snare and Bass Drums... Play all sixteenth notes as even strokes.

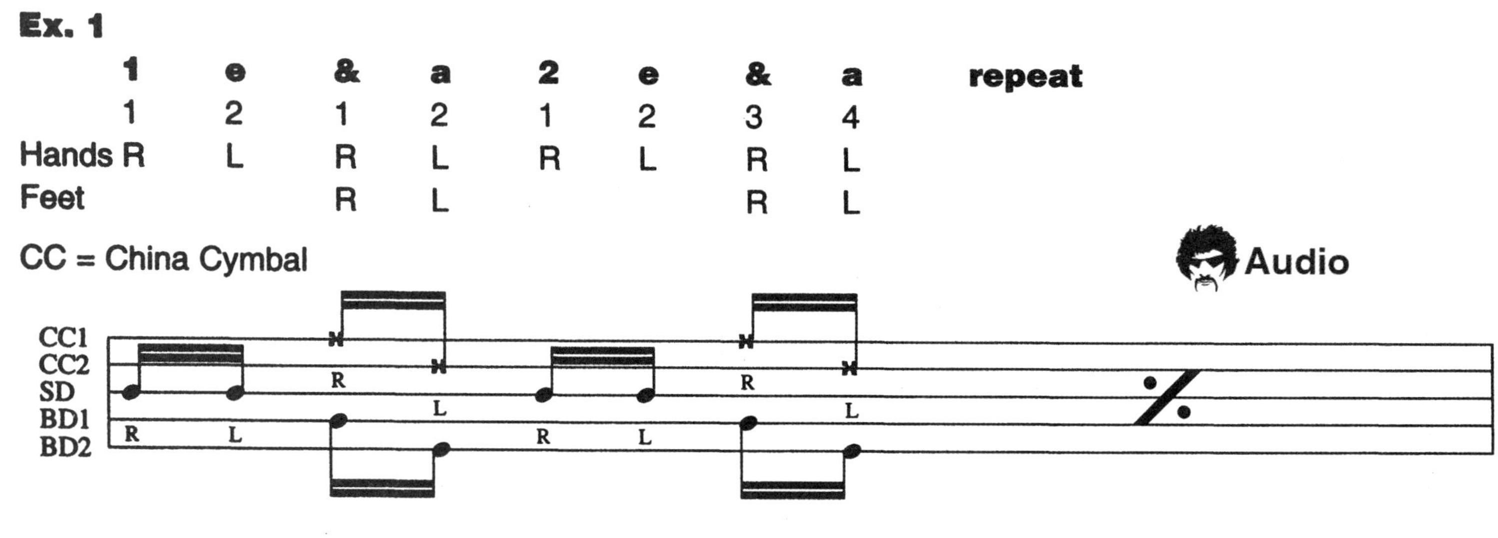

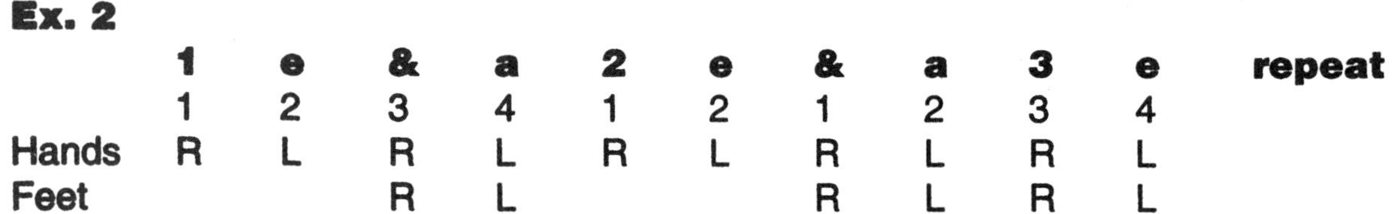

Ex. 2

	1	e	&	a	2	e	&	a	3	e	repeat
	1	2	3	4	1	2	1	2	3	4	
Hands	R	L	R	L	R	L	R	L	R	L	
Feet			R	L			R	L	R	L	

Play these slow at first then build up speed. After you build up speed... Practice playing the hands and feet together with the China cymbals. (See Below)

Audio

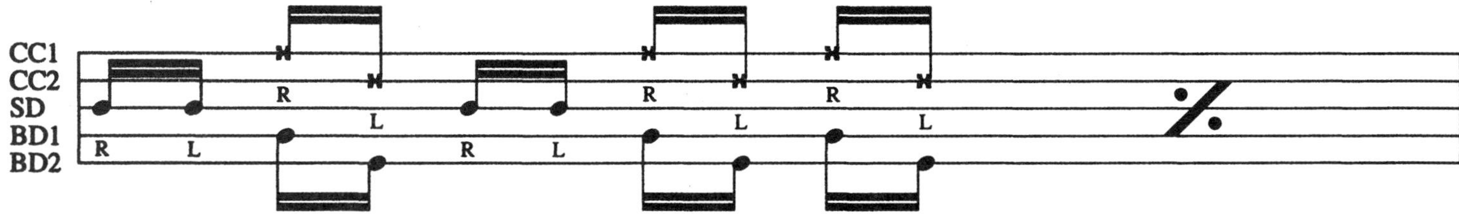

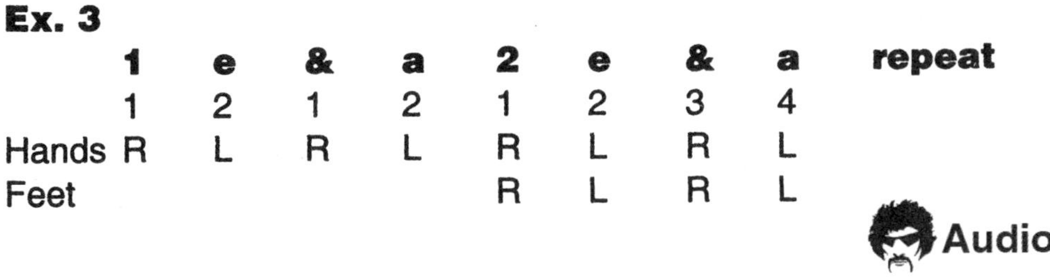

Ex. 3

	1	**e**	**&**	**a**	**2**	**e**	**&**	**a**	**repeat**
	1	2	1	2	1	2	3	4	
Hands	R	L	R	L	R	L	R	L	
Feet					R	L	R	L	

Audio

Combinations with Triplets

Audio

Play evenly as triplets.

Practice slowly at first and build up speed!

Ex. 1

	1	**&**	**a**	**2**	**&**	**a**	**3**	**&**	**a**	**4**	**&**	**a**
	1	2	3	1	2	3	1	2	3	1	2	3
Hands	R	L	R				R	L	R			
Feet				R	L	R				R	L	R

Ex. 2

	1	**&**	**a**	**2**	**&**	**a**	**3**	**&**	**a**	**4**	**&**	**a**
	1	2	3	1	2	3	1	2	3	1	2	3
Hands	R	L			R	L			R	L		
Feet			R	L			R	L			R	L

Ex. 3

	1	**&**	**a**	**2**	**&**	**a**	**3**	**&**	**a**	**4**	**&**	**a**
	1	2	3	1	2	3	1	2	3	1	2	3
Hands	L	R	L				L	R	L			
Feet				R	L	R				R	L	R

Note: Play **Ex. 2** with the **R L** on the feet together with the China cymbals.

Ex. 4

	1	&	a	2	&	a	3	&	a	4	&	a
Hands	L	R	L	R	L	R	L	R	L	R	L	R
Feet				R	L	R				R	L	R

L R L R L R L R L R L R

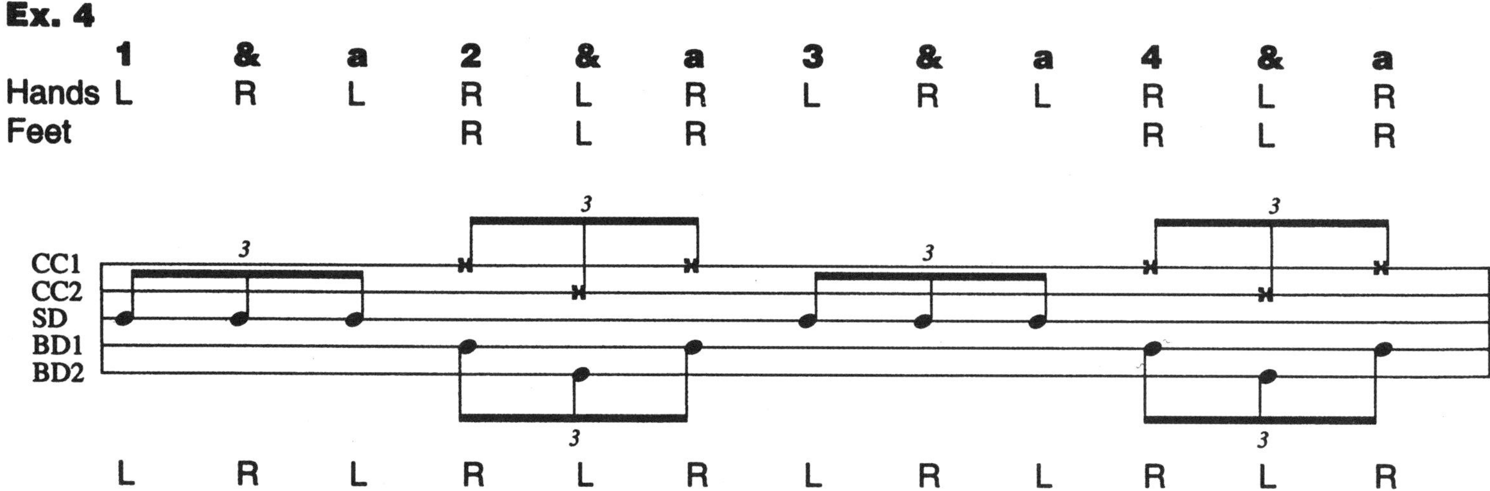

LISTEN TO THE **FILL** IN THE **AUDIO FILES.**

The China cymbals are to be played together with the bass drums.

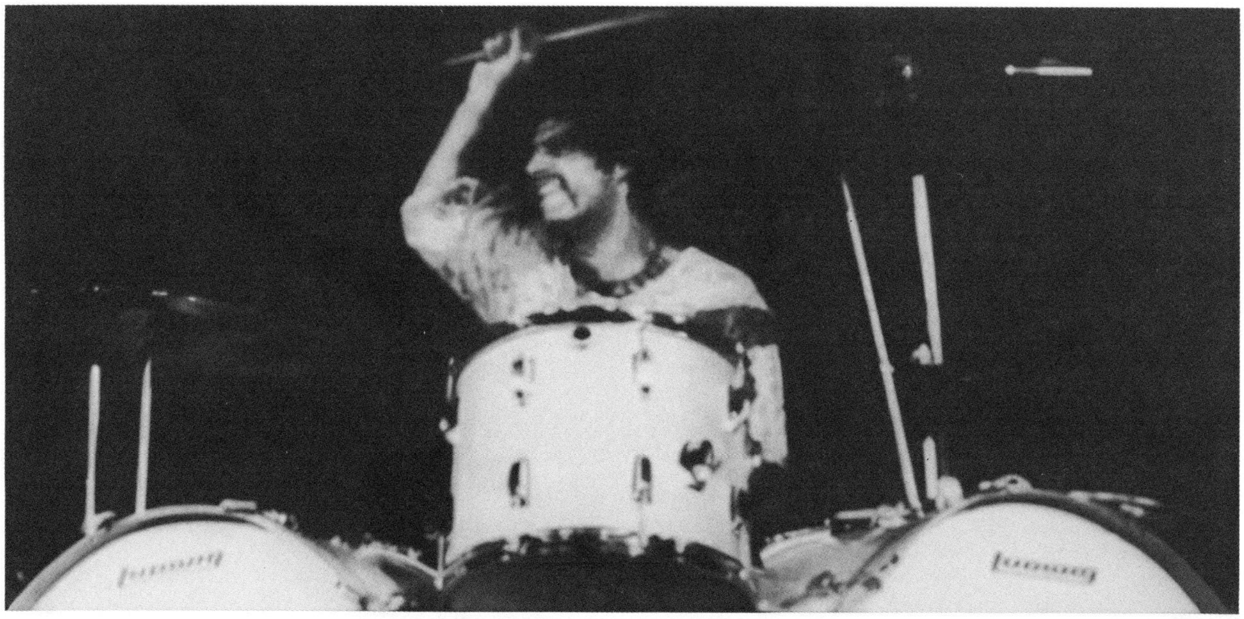

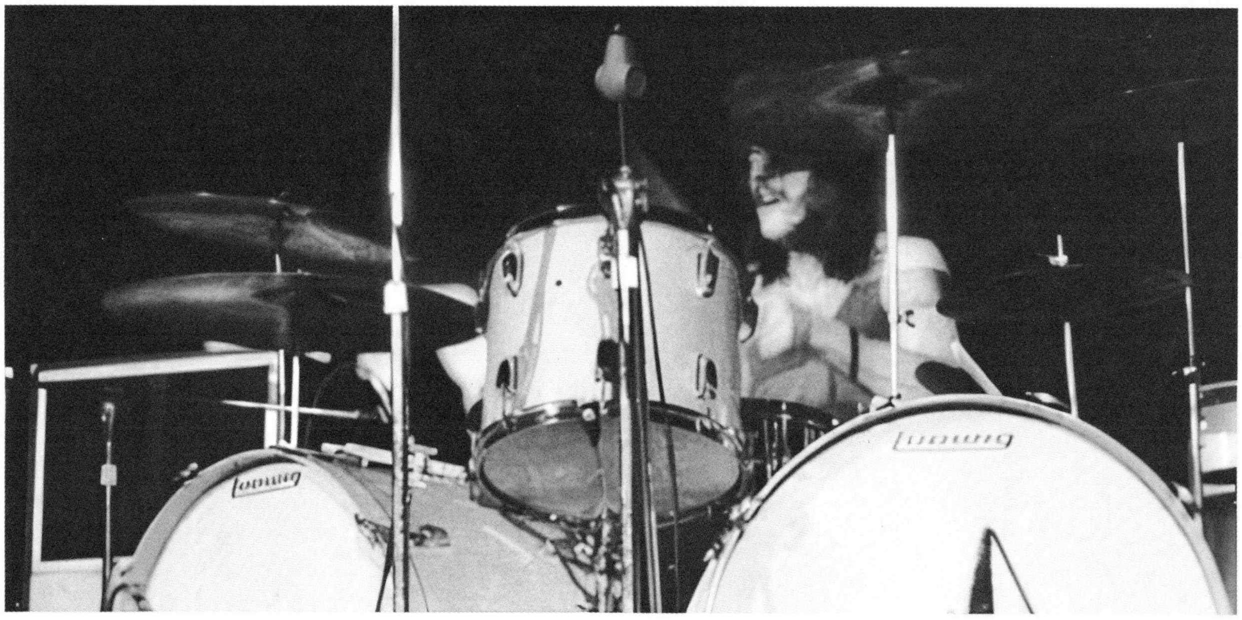

Carmine got Ludwig to send identical drum kits to himself (top) and John Bonham (bottom). Here are both drummers in action with these drums; this was the only time Bonzo played double bass drums.

Part 17

Audio

Pop / Dance

Here are some of the basic **Pop** patterns played today. The opening and closing Hi-Hat and the steady quarter notes on the bass drum are the "trademark" of these rhythms. Practice at **160** Tempos or more!

+ = closed Hi-Hat
0 = open Hi-Hat

1. + 0 + + + 0 + +
HH
SD
BD

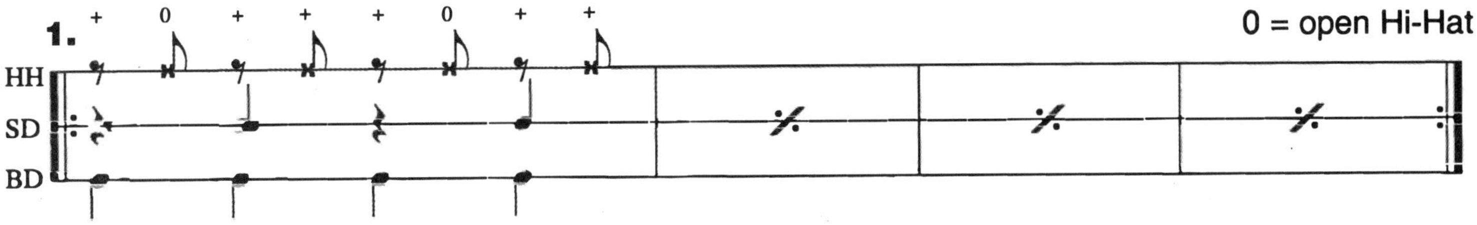

2. + 0 + + + 0 + +
HH
SD
BD

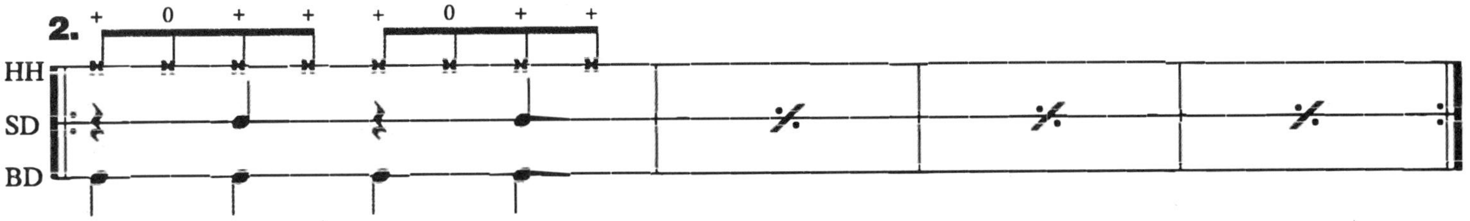

3. + + + 0 + + + 0
HH
SD
BD

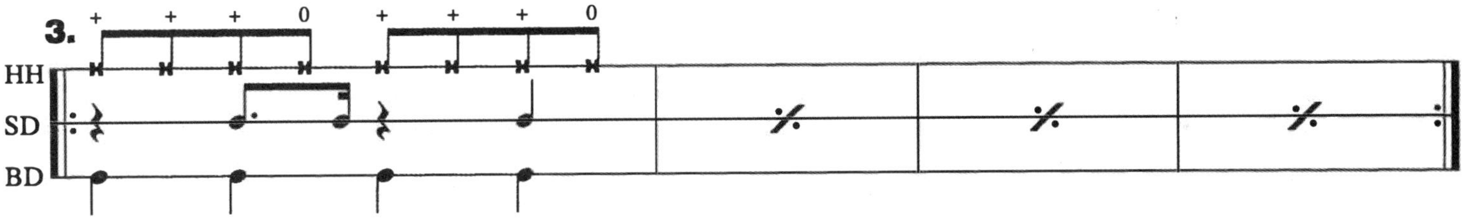

4. > > > >
HH
SD
BD

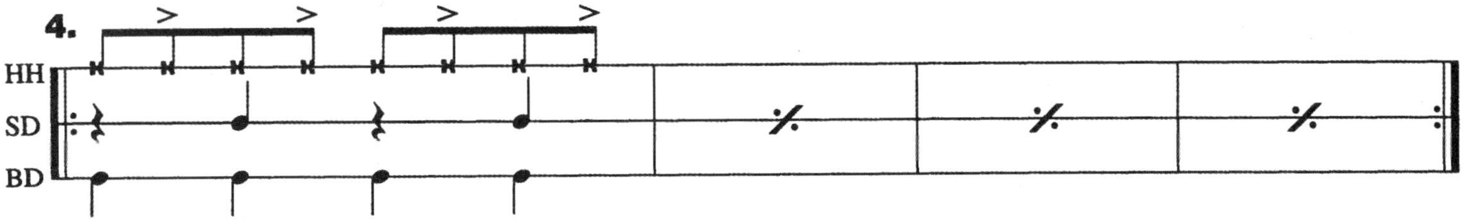

5. + 0 + + + 0 + +
HH
SD
BD

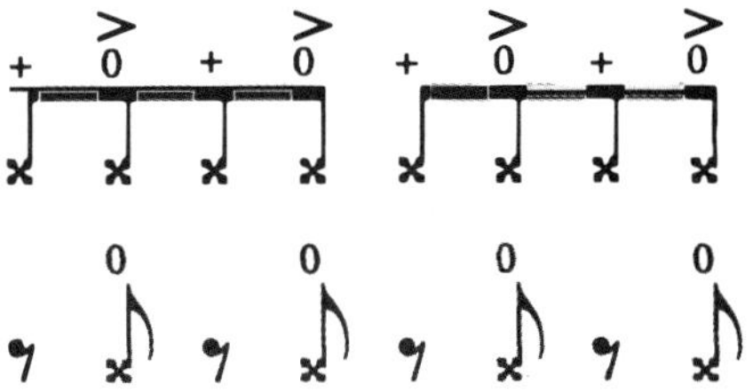

+ 0 + 0 + 0 + 0

0 0 0 0

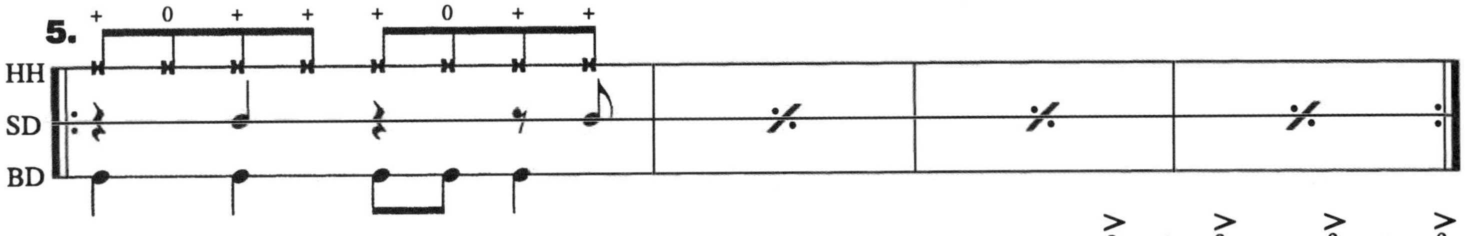

Note: Practice all of the exercises opening the Hi-Hat on all the **upbeats** or **&'s** with these two examples.

Realistic Drum Fills: Replacements

The following pages are excerpted from my book *Realistic Drum Fills: Replacements*, available through Hudson Music. The book will develop your ability to play cool drum fills and solo ideas. It covers a technique I call "replacements," where you replace notes played by the hand with notes played by the foot on the bass drum. I've been using this concept for many years and have seen many of my idols using it before me. Greats like Buddy Rich, Gene Krupa, Max Roach, Louis Bellson, and Billy Cobham (as well as many modern players) all use these kinds of replacements in their playing.

This book puts these concepts into a learning program that keeps progressing to the next (more difficult) level, moving from eighth notes to triplets and 16ths, which gets you playing different pulsations of these concepts. As in my other books, I'll always present 10-12 individual exercises, and then I will present a 6-, 8-, 12-, or 16-bar exercise putting all the patterns together side by side. This demonstrates how these patterns work together to develop solo ideas and create melodic drum patterns. These replacements can be used in rock, jazz, Latin, or just about any other kind of music.

The pages included here show a taste of the basic eighth-note, triplet, and 16th-note replacements, followed by some fills that apply the concept to the full kit within a 4-bar groove phrase.

To learn more of these fills, check out the full version of ***Realistic Drum Fills: Replacements***!

Key To Replacements Section

> = Accents: I like to use rim shots for accents on the drums and pad.

(F) = Bass Drum

[R] or [L] = the strokes being replaced.

HH = Hi-Hat

RC = Ride Cymbal

SD = Snare Drum

TT = Small Tom

FT = Floor Tom

Example

Whenever you see an (F) in the sticking, this indicates that you should leave out the hand stroke and replace it with a note on the bass drum. Play the note with the (F) under it on the bass drum while playing the original sticking. The (F) replaces the right hand on beat 1.

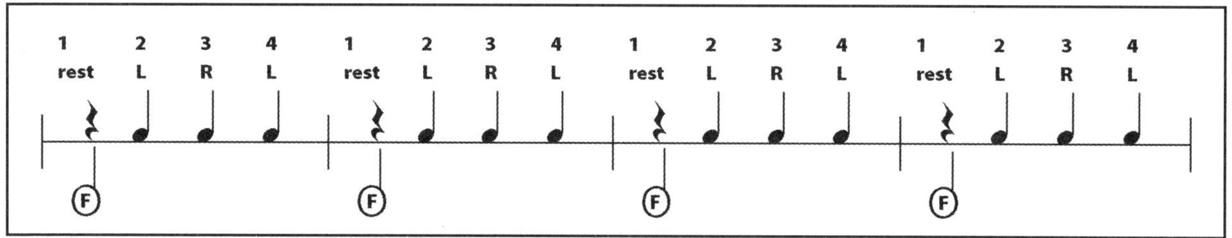

So on beat 1, instead of playing the right hand, you will play the bass drum instead. Then the sticking continues and plays the L R L on the counts of 2, 3, and 4. This repeats 3 times to make it a 4-bar phrase.

Many exercises have 2 or more stickings to practice. Be sure to practice all of them carefully.

Section 1: Eighth-Note Combinations

As indicated in the key to the book, the Ⓕ is the right foot on the bass drum (left foot for lefty drummers) and the R is the sticking being replaced.

1 + 2 +
Ⓕ L R L
[R]

Throughout the book there are certain exercises where the replaced sticking is shown in a box underneath the exercise. These boxed strokes are eliminated and replaced with bass drum notes.

So, in this first section, the replacements work like this: the Ⓕ on beat 1 means that the bass drum replaces the right hand stroke on that count. Then the rest of the pattern is played as written with L-R-L sticking on counts "& 2 &."

Eventually we drop the replaced sticking notation and just use the Ⓕ to show that the bass drum plays that note.

Remember to do all these exercises slowly at first and gradually build up speed on each pattern. Play the patterns over and over. Watch the two different stickings and the note being replaced. Playing both stickings is important, so make sure you give them both equal practicing time.

As the book progresses, the sticking will change to mixed sticking: some sticking will not alternate. These changes will create new melodic replacement patterns.

Let's get started!

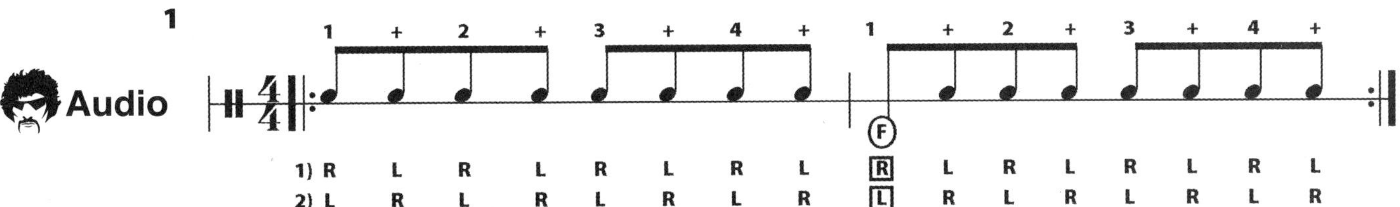

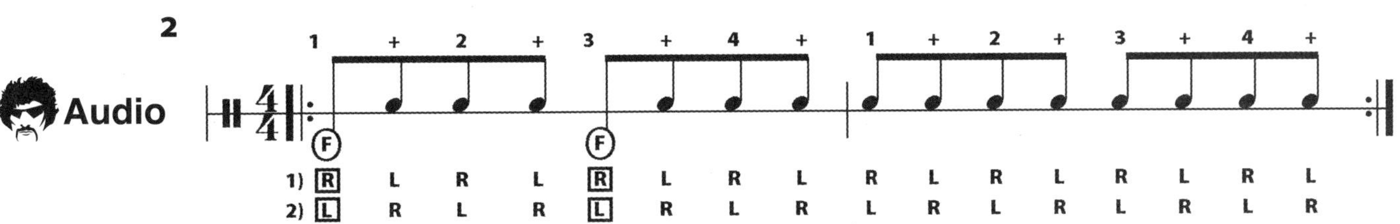

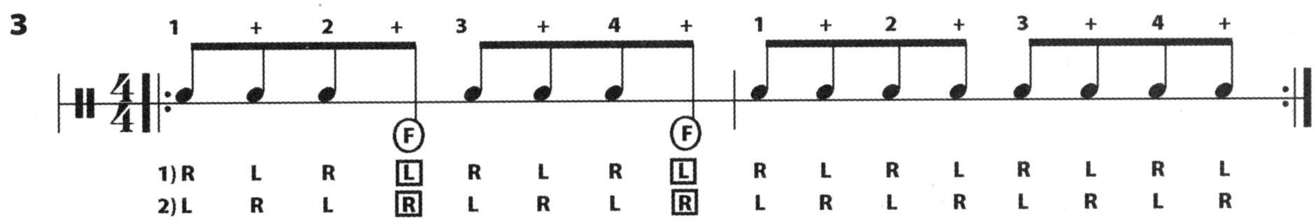

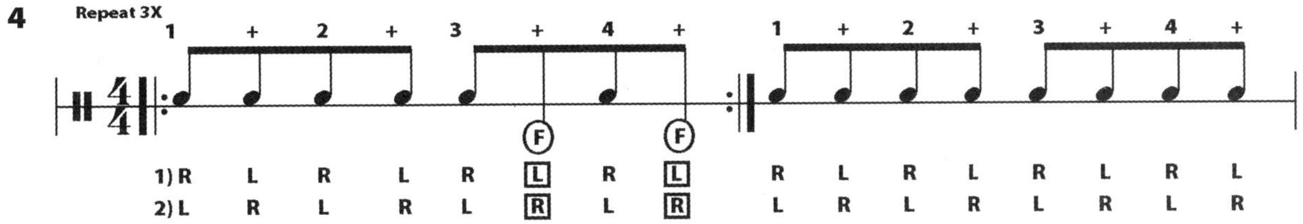

5
Repeat 3X
1 + 2 + 3 + 4 + 1 + 2 + 3 + 4 +
1) R L R L R L R L R L R L R L R L
2) L R L R L R L R
6
Audio
Repeat 3X
1 + 2 + 3 + 4 + 1 + 2 + 3 + 4 +
1) R L R L R L R L R L R L R L R L
2) L R L R L R L R L R L R L R L R
7
Repeat 3X
1 + 2 + 3 + 4 + 1 + 2 + 3 + 4 +
1) R L R L R L R L R L R L R L R L
2) L R L R L R L R L R L R L R L R
8
Repeat 3X
1 + 2 + 3 + 4 + 1 + 2 + 3 + 4 +
1) R L R L R L R L R L R L R L R L
2) L R L R L R L R L R L R L R L R
9
Audio
Repeat 3X
1 + 2 + 3 + 4 + 1 + 2 + 3 + 4 +
1) R L R L R L R L R L R L R L R L
2) L R L R L R L R L R L R L R L R
10
1 + 2 + 3 + 4 + 1 + 2 + 3 + 4 +
1) R L R L R L R L R L R L R L R L
2) L R L R L R L R L R L R L R L R

Section 2: Replacement Triplets

Here we continue our studies with the replacement concept. On these exercises we are just using the (F) on the count that is being replaced.

So, in a triplet pattern it looks like this:

Example:

1 + A 2 + A 3 + A 4 + A
3 3 3 3
F L R L R L R L R L R L

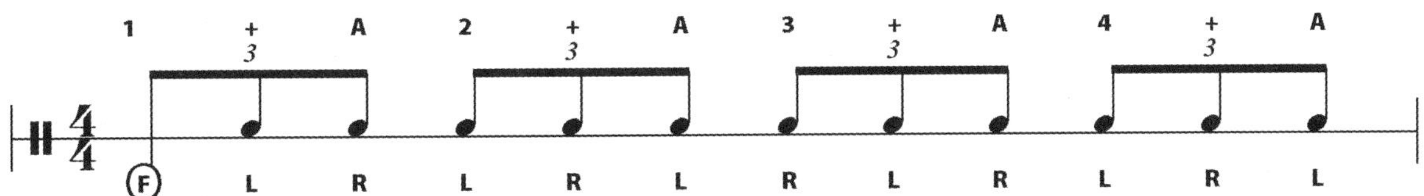

The foot is on the count of "1" while the hands play the triplet with alternate sticking. These triplets sound great. Watch for the patterns with the accents (>); they are really cool and very melodic.

Have fun. Play slow at first and build speed.

Triplet Exercises

1

Audio

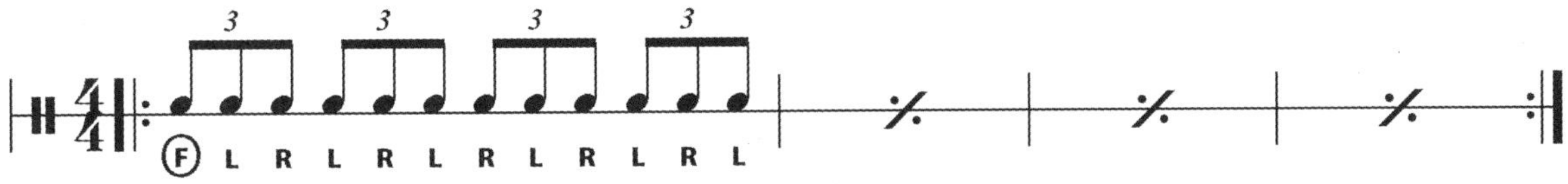

F L R L R L R L R L R L

2

Audio

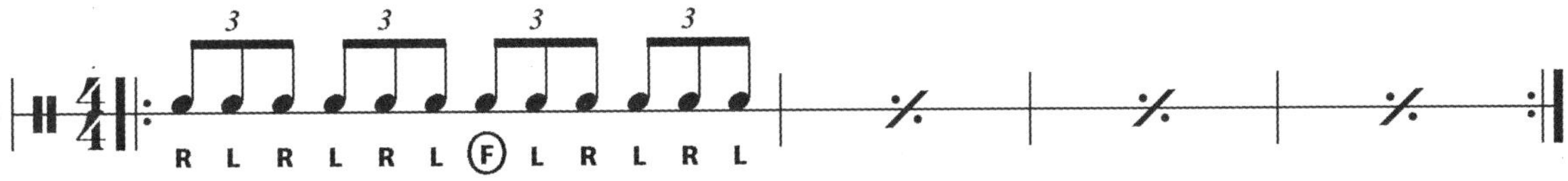

R L R L R L F L R L R L

3

R L R F R L R L R L R L

4

R L R L R L R L R F R L

5

F L R F R L R L R L R L

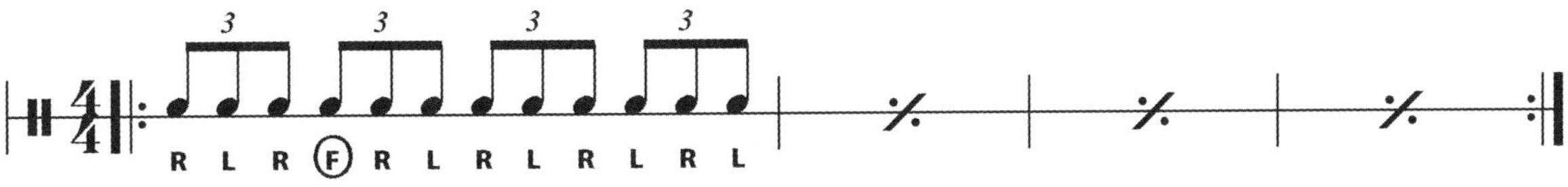

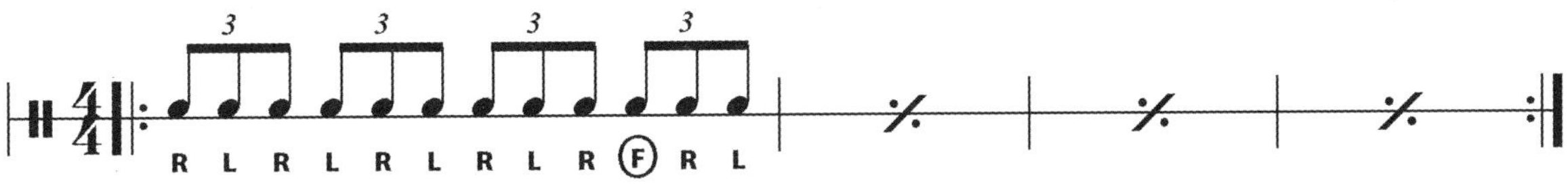

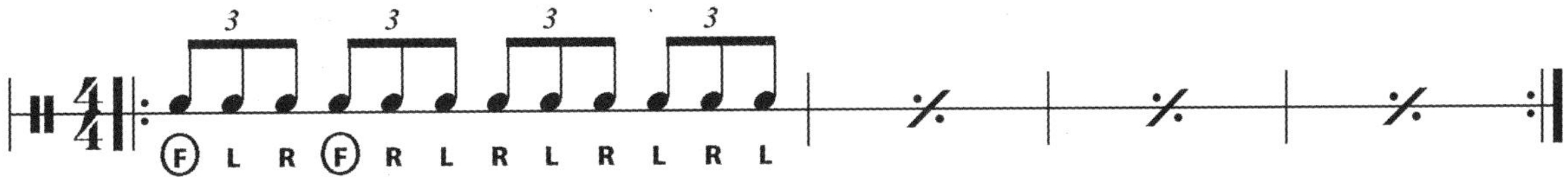

Section 3: Replacement Sixteenth Notes

Next we'll look at sixteenth notes, starting simply by replacing the downbeats in the 16-note flow.

Practice these slowly at first and don't try to go too fast right away. You must make sure all your strokes sound even. Don't forget to try reverse the written stickings.

From this point forward in the book, only the right-hand lead sticking is shown, but you should also continue to practice left-hand stickings as well. Simply reverse the sticking show and practice it that way as well.

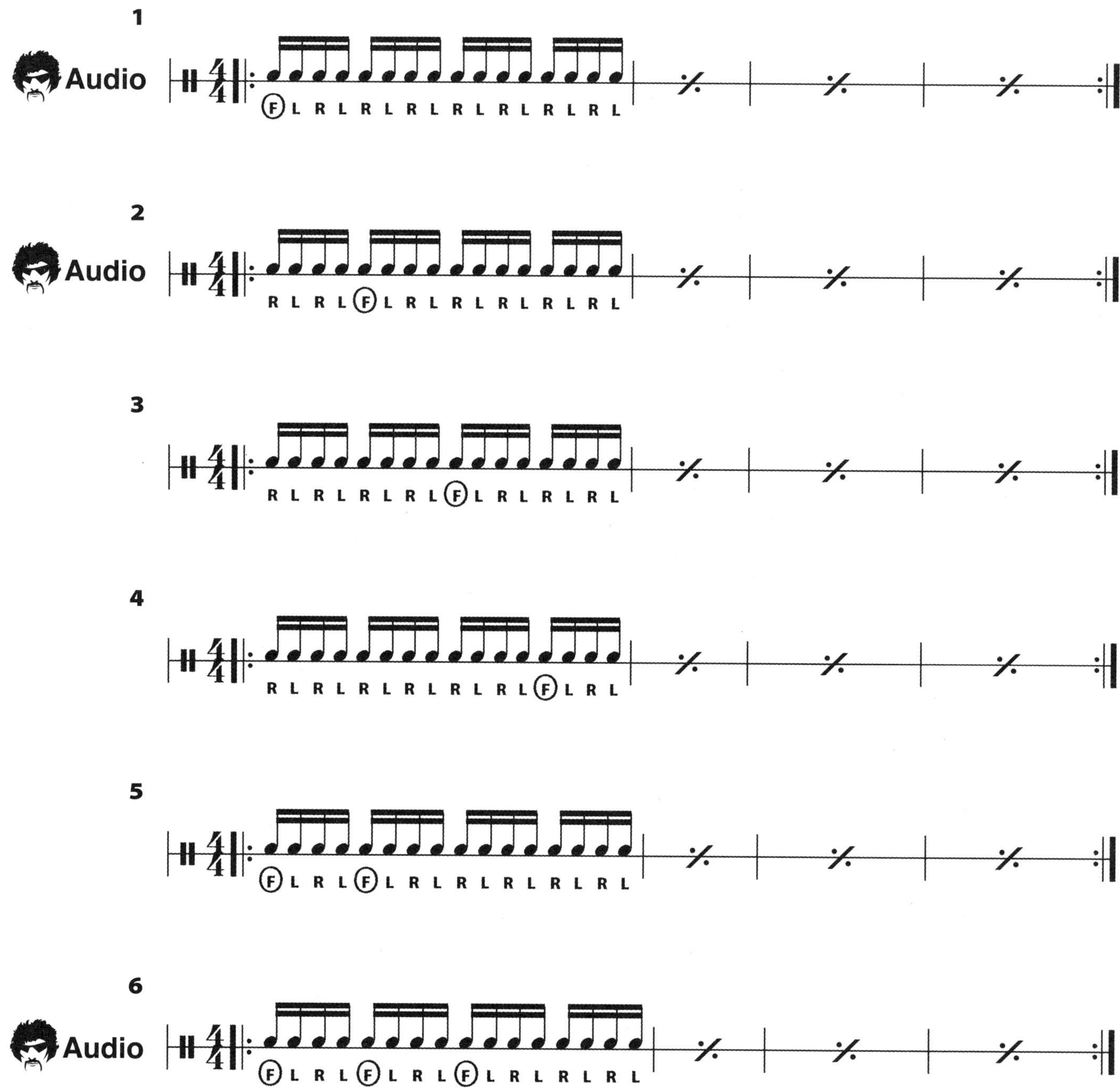

Replacement Drum Fills

Here we play 2 or 3 bars of rock grooves and then we play a replacement drum fill on the kit. These are fun to play, and can be used for drum fills to play in your band. Also included in these sections are drum fills played in a shuffle groove (dotted eighth and sixteenth). These are fun and different to play than an eighth-note groove.

Look at the groove and the fill and make the drum fills swing. Have fun!!

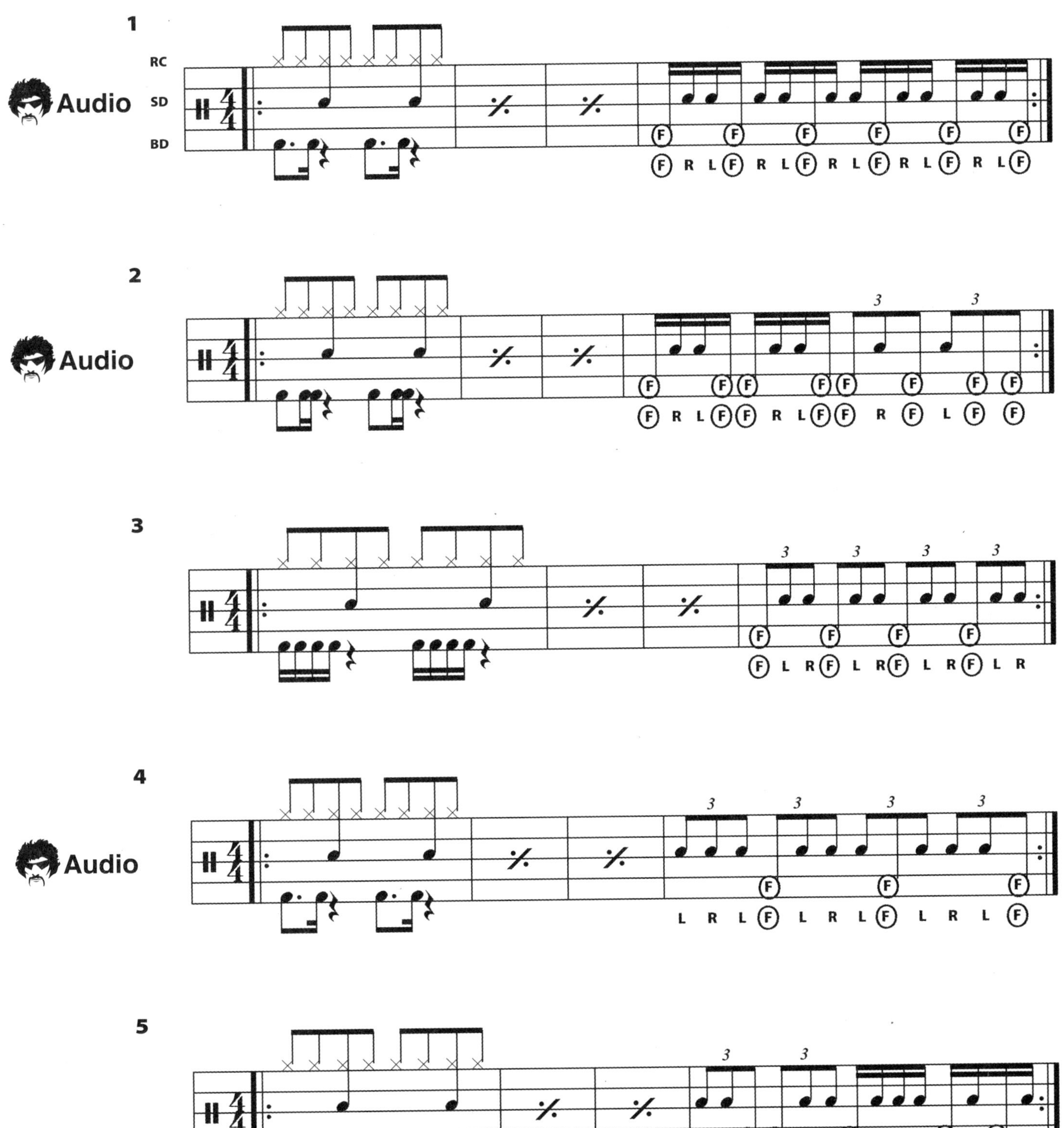

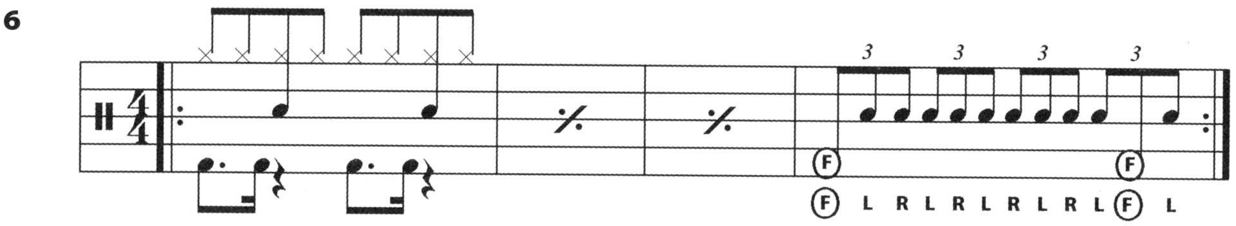
6
3 3 3 3
F L R L R L R L R L F L

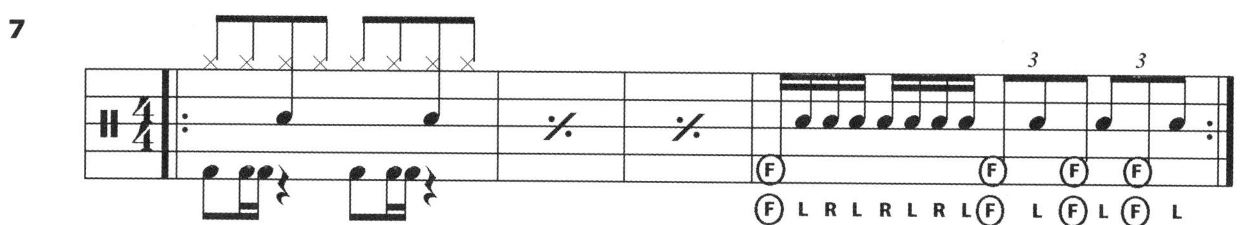
7
3 3
F L R L R L R L F L F L F L

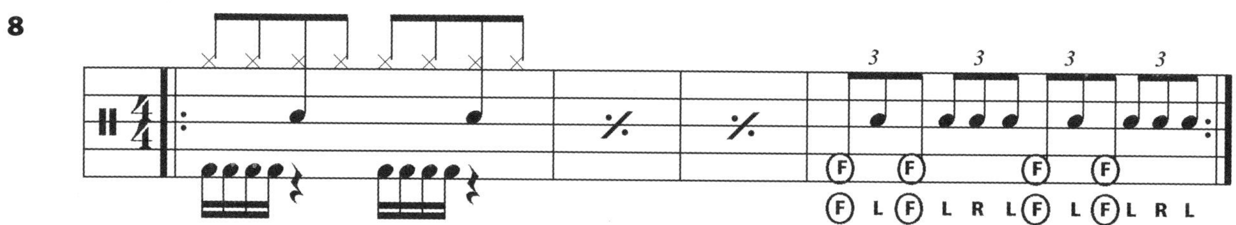
8
3 3 3 3
F L F L R L F L F L R L

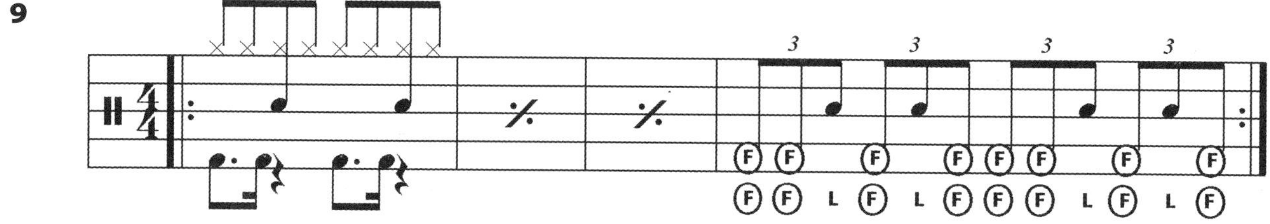
9
3 3 3 3
F F L F L F F F L F L F

DISCOGRAPHY

Artist	Album	Record Label
Vanilla Fudge	Vanilla Fudge	Atco/Atlantic
Vanilla Fudge	The Beat Goes On	Atco/Atlantic
Vanilla Fudge	Renaissance	Atco/Atlantic
Vanilla Fudge	Near the Beginning	Atco/Atlantic
Vanilla Fudge	Rock and Roll	Atco/Atlantic
Vanilla Fudge	2001	Hyperspace
Vanilla Fudge	Mystery	Atco
Vanilla Fudge	Live, Best of	Rhino
Vanilla Fudge	Out Through the In Door	
Cactus	Cactus	Atco/Atlantic
Cactus	One Way or Another	Atco/Atlantic
Cactus	Restrictions	Atco/Atlantic
Cactus	'Ot 'N Sweaty	Atco/Atlantic
Cactus	Collection/Cactology	Rhino
Cactus	Cactus Music/Cacuts V plus DVD	Fuel
Jeff Beck, Tim Bogert, Carmine Appice	Beck, Bogert & Appice	Epic/CBS
Jeff Beck	Beckology	Epic
KGB	KGB	MCA
KGB	Motion	MCA
Rod Stewart & Group	Foot Loose & Fancy Free	Warner Bros.
Rod Stewart & Group	Blondes Have More Fun	Warner Bros.
Rod Stewart & Group	Foolish Behavior	Warner Bros.
Rod Stewart & Group	Tonight I'm Yours	Warner Bros.
Rod Stewart	Rod Stewart Anthology	Geffen
Stanley Clarke	Modern Man	CBS
Paul Stanley	Kiss – Paul Stanley	Casablanca/Polygram
Ron Wood	1, 2, 3, 4	CBS
Carmine Appice	Carmine Appice/Rockers	Pasha/CBS
Carmine Appice	Channel Mind Radio	Polydor KK
Carmine Appice	Guitar Zeus I	Apollion, No Bull (Europe)
Carmine Appice	Guitar Zeus II	
Carmine Appice	Guitar Zeus (Japan)	Rock Records (Japan)
Carmine Appice	Guitar Zeus Conquering Heroes	Fuel
Ted Nugent	Nugent	Atlantic
King Kobra	Ready to Strike	Capitol
King Kobra	Thrill of a Lifetime	Capitol
King Kobra	King Kobra III	Rocker
King Kobra	Lost Years	Cleopatra Records
King Kobra	Hollywood Trash	MTM (Europe)
King Kobra	TBA	Fuel
Soundtrack/TriStar	Iron Eagle	Capitol
Pink Floyd	Momentary Lapse of Reason	CBS
Blue Murder	Blue Murder	Geffen
Blue Murder	Nothin' but Trouble	Geffen
Brad Gillis	Gillrock Ranch	Guitar Recordings
Jeff Watson	Lone Ranger	Shrapnel
Mothers Army	Mothers Army (Japan)	Appollion (Fems)
Pearl	East Meets West	Polydor KK
Pearl	4 Infinity	East West
Pearl	Live in Japan	Distribute/Sony
Char, Bogert & Appice	CBA Live in Japan	Polydor KK
Derringer & Appice	Party Tested	Boardwalk Records
Derringer, Bogert & Appice	DBA Doin' Business As	SPV (Europe)
Travers & Appice	It Takes a Lot of Balls	
Travers & Appice	Live – Keep on Rockin'	Fuel

DISCOGRAPHY (cont.)

Artist	Album	Record Label
Appice Perdomo Project	Energy Overload (Instrumental)	Cleopatra Records
Appice Perdomo Project	Running up the Hill	Cleopatra Records
Beck Bogert Appice	Box Set Live	Rhino
Cactus	Tightrope	Cleopatra Records
Cactus	Temple of Blues 1 & 2	Cleopatra Records
Carmine Appice	Guitar Zeus Box Set	Deko Entertainment
Carmine Appice/Vinny Appice: Appice Brothers	Sinister	SPV Records
King Kobra	We are Warriors	Cleopatra Records
King Kobra	King Kobra	Frontiers Music SRL
King Kobra	Have a Good Time	Frontiers Music SRL
King Kobra	Live at Sweden Rock Festival	Frontiers Music SRL
Rated X (Joe Lynn Turner, Carmine Appice, Tony Franklin)	Rated X	Frontiers Music SRL
Vanilla Fudge	Spirit of 67	Cleopatra Records

Books

Stick It! My Life of Sex, Drums, and Rock 'n' Roll by Carmine Appice (autobiography)

ENDORSEMENTS

Audix Microphones
Calzone/Anvil Cases
Canopus Products
ddrum Drums
DW Pedals & Hardware
Evans Drumheads
Gator Cases
Puresound Snare Wires
Sabian Cymbals
Vic Firth Signature Sticks

PERFORMANCE SET-UP

ddrum Drums

- Two 24" x 14" bass drums; 12" x 8" and 13" x 9" rack toms; 16" x 16" and 16" x 18" floor toms
- 14" x 5" Carmine Appice Signature brass snare drum
- 15" Carmine Appice "Shade" cymbal

Sabian Cymbals

- 17" and 19" Carmine Appice Signature Chinas
- 21" Carmine Appice Signature ride
- 18" and 20" HH crashes
- 14" HH hi-hats

DW Pedals

- 5000 Series single and double pedals
- Hardware

For more information about Carmine Appice, including tour dates, audio, video and more, go to www.carmineappice.com or www.carmineappice.net.

For t-shirts, autographs, photos, CDs, sticks, vinyl, artwork, and more, go to: www.CarmineMerch.com

Carmine was thrilled and honored to do a drum clinic with his two idols, Buddy Rich and Joe Morello, in 1978.
Courtesy of the Charley Braun Collection

Carmine Then and Now.